IATEFL

36th International Annual Conference
York, 24–27 March 2002

Edited by Alan Pulverness

Editorial Committee: Jonathan Marks, Amos Paran, Silvana Richardson

iatefl

Published by IATEFL, 3 Kingsdown Chambers,
Kingsdown Park, Whitstable, Kent CT5 2DJ

First published 2002

British Library Cataloguing in Publication Data
Education
Pulverness, Alan (Ed.)
IATEFL 2002 York Conference Selections

ISBN 1 901095 11 8

For a complete list of IATEFL publications, please
write to the above address, or visit the IATEFL
website at www.iatefl.org

IATEFL Publications Officer: Jonathan Marks. Copy-edited by Sue Harmes.
Designed and typeset by Keith Rigley, Charlbury.
Printed in Britain by Information Press, Eynsham.

CONTENTS

EDITOR'S INTRODUCTION

For its *36th International Annual Conference* the IATEFL was back in York for the first time since 1995. By contrast with the city settings and conference hotels of Dublin 2000 and Brighton 2001, this year's conference also marked a return to the relative seclusion of a university campus, where the reflective peace was disturbed only by the insistent squawking of ducks on the lake …

With four days of concurrent sessions, one of the first things that delegates need to do once they have registered is to plan their individual pathways through a varied and extensive programme. Brief abstracts and a coded classification system offer some direction, but this year it was possible to make all those invidious choices well in advance by downloading the 80-page programme from the IATEFL website. Notable innovations at the conference itself were two extended debates, on ELT publishing and graded readers, both of which are reported in Chapter 6. The conference also saw the genesis of the fifteenth Special Interest Group for members interested in or involved with ESOL.

This year's conference was well punctuated by Plenary talks dealing with a number of major areas – method, language, learner autonomy, teacher development and task-based instruction – that provided several *leitmotifs* for the week and provoked widespread debate. B. Kumaravadivelu's opening Plenary gave a synoptic overview of professional thinking that summarised a history of method and the 'antimethod' reaction in the 1980s against the whole concept of method, before identifying a current postmodern condition of 'postmethod'. Questioning the notion of principled eclecticism as rarely being guided by coherent and responsible principles, Kumaravadivelu proposed an open but rigorous framework, informed by parameters of appropriateness to local conditions ('particularity'), practice-led theory ('practicality') and critical pedagogy ('possibility'), which generates a set of ten macrostrategies. As he points out, these are not intended to be prescriptive, but rather should be understood as 'general operating strategies' whose realisation will vary according to particular circumstances. They suggest quite powerfully, however, what the principles of a responsible and truly principled eclecticism might be. Kumaravadivelu also reports on his workshop on Fostering Language Awareness, in which he illustrated one aspect of the parameter of possibility, demonstrating some sample microstrategies involving critical reading and critical language awareness that could be applied in the service of one macrostrategy.

Diane Larsen-Freeman began her Plenary talk by proposing ten views of the nature of language, and proceeded to examine the relationship between some of these perspectives on language and their realisation in differential theories of learning and teaching. Diane echoed Kumaravadivelu's concern with influential contextual factors, acknowledging the fact that such theories may overlap and coalesce, producing idiosyncratic varieties of combinatory practices. Then, drawing on a constructivist paradigm of 'inert' vs 'dynamic' knowledge, she went on to explore ways in which language can be viewed as a dynamic system, in terms of change over time, online processing and decision-making, and (most relevantly for the classroom) borrowing from descriptions of phenomena in the natural world, as an 'emergent' means of making meaning. The emergentist position suggests a view of grammar as a dynamic system created and progressively adapted by users of the language rather than an inert or static body of knowledge to be acquired and adhered to. Other reports in Chapter 2 focus on the use of corpus data, on Conversational Analysis and on ellipsis, neglected in published materials, and therefore neglected in classrooms, too, thereby suggesting a number of ways in which the dynamic and variable nature of language may be reflected in more open and flexible methodologies. Some important caveats about corpora are raised, however, in Hugh Dellar's provocatively-titled report 'What have corpora ever done for us?'

Learner autonomy, like communicative language teaching, is something that most teachers profess to believe in, though in practice its scope is sometimes restricted to promoting independence for students for as long as they are students. In the Plenary talk that opens Chapter 3, Leni Dam took a longer view, seeing learner autonomy not as an end in itself, but as orientation for lifelong learning. Leni provided specific examples to illustrate the transformative effect of the shift from teacher- and teaching-centred to learner- and learning-centred approaches, on teacher and learner roles, on lesson content, and on the classroom itself. Several short transcripts of classroom exchanges reinforce Kumaravadivelu's concern with particularity, as well as Diane Larsen-Freeman's concept of dynamism, pointing to the unpredictable quality of language that emerges naturally when the agenda is set by the learner. Leni also reminded us that encouraging learners to become more autonomous is not an easy option: she acknowledged some of the problems that may arise and concluded by emphasising the teacher's responsibility for preparing learners to assume responsibility for their own learning. Other reports in Chapter 3 amplify the theme, with various accounts of learner-centred practice, including collaborative learning, peer support in using the Web, a framework for assessing one's own learning style, and the use of reflective journals as a tool for learners to monitor improvements in pronunciation.

While Leni was addressing the issue of learner autonomy, elsewhere on the campus in a concurrent Plenary, Martha Pennington investigated 'Personal Teaching Frameworks' and the way in which these mental models may be modified, destabilised, or remain unaffected by the introduction of innovations. Martha first identified a range of 'paradoxes, contrasting priorities, and gaps' and characterised teaching as a constant balancing act, attempting to maintain equilibrium, to bridge the gaps between various binary oppositions. She then described a cline of responses to innovation, ranging from the uncritical, 'spontaneous' adoption of the novice teacher to the 'habitual maintenance of one's tried-and-true teaching framework' by the old hand. Once again, there was an echo of the flexibility and openness of Kumaravadivelu's postmethod parameters: Martha's analysis of ways in which change occurs (or fails to occur) will certainly be resonant for anyone involved in teacher education, but her concluding remarks were reassuringly inconclusive, reminding us that teachers 'need to learn to live in the dialectic tension that knows no perfect solution, no right or wrong'. In addition to a number of reports on specific topics in teacher training and teacher development, Simon Borg and Costas Gabrielatos look at the nature of the language teacher and language teaching, while Brian Winn-Smith raises some important concerns on quality issues in the proliferating field of distance programmes.

Chapter 5 brings together a variety of reports on instructional approaches, ranging from the use of Cuisenaire rods to content-and-language integrated learning and from teachers singing and miming to the use of TV commercials. Charles Hadfield takes us back to basics, reminding us of what can be achieved in the 'lo-tech' classroom, while Derrin Kent presents a lesson-planning framework within the perspective of Task-Based Learning. This chapter is introduced by Peter Skehan's closing Plenary, a detailed study of task-based instruction in terms of theory, research and practice. Theory and research are often seen in opposition to, or at least as separate from, practice, producing what Kumaravadivelu calls 'an unfortunate and unproductive division of labour between the theorist and the teacher', but in this case it was clear that there were valuable insights to be gained from research findings, particularly as regards the predictability of certain task-types and the balance between task performance and focus on form.

Both the debates, on publishing and graded readers, were well attended and discussion was wide-ranging and far more convergent than some people had feared it might be. The debates are represented in Chapter 6, with statements and comments from the main speakers. Thanks to Jill Florent and Philip Prowse for their help in putting these reports together. Finally, in Chapter 7, there are two 'voices from the floor' in reviews of the conference by delegates from Estonia and Germany.

It would not be possible to produce the *Conference Selections* without the support of the editorial committee (Jonathan Marks and Amos Paran, joined this year by Silvana Richardson), who once again this year have had the task of reading a prodigious number of short reports, far more than can be represented in this publication. Thanks, too, to Sue Harmes, the Editor's editor!

NOTE: Bibliographies and references are given in full for Plenary papers, but are not included with short reports. Readers wishing to follow up bibliographical references can obtain the relevant details on application to the authors, or to the editor in cases where no contact information is given.

Alan Pulverness
Norwich Institute for Language Education, September 2002

Shortly before this edition of *Selections* went to print, we received the very sad news that Gillian Porter Ladousse had died. For many years Gillian played a key role in both the Literature and Cultural Studies and the Teacher Trainers and Educators SIGs. She then served as the SIG representative on the main IATEFL committee. At the York conference, she chaired the publishing debate, which she had convened (together with Alan Maley), and the success and vitality of that event is a small tribute to her commitment and creative energy. She will be greatly missed by everyone who knew her.

1 OPENING PLENARY

1.1 Method, antimethod, postmethod

B. Kumaravadivelu *San José State University, California, USA*

The purpose of this paper is to deconstruct the existing concept of method, describe the prevailing antimethod sentiments, and delineate the emerging postmethod condition. The paper is divided into three parts. In the first, I present a critical appraisal of the limited and limiting nature of the concept of method. In the second, I describe how widespread dissatisfaction with established methods created and sustained antimethod sentiments among teachers and teacher educators. In the third, I discuss how a state of heightened awareness about the futility of searching for the right method has resulted in the emergence of what I have called a postmethod condition. I conclude the paper by presenting the essentials of a postmethod pedagogy, and by pointing out the potential it has for shaping and reshaping the fundamental character of second and foreign (L2) language teaching and teacher education.

Method

The concept of method in language teaching is perhaps as old as the history of language teaching itself. It has for long guided the form and function of every conceivable component of language teaching, including curriculum design, syllabus specifications, materials preparation, instructional strategies and testing techniques. All of us hear and use the term *method* very often. Yet, we hardly pause to think about its meaning.

What does method actually mean? Nearly forty years ago, William Mackey asked the same question and lamented that the word *method* 'means so little and so much' (1965: 139). The reason for this, he said, 'lies in the state and organization of our knowledge of language and language learning. It lies in wilful ignorance of what has been done and said and thought in the past. It lies in the vested interests which methods become. It lies in the meaning of method' (ibid). What he said nearly four decades ago is still true today.

We generally use the term *method* to refer to the theoretical principles and classroom practices that we read about in methods textbooks. We also use the term to refer to what practising teachers actually do in their classrooms. What the books say is different from what the teachers do, even though we use the same term, *method*, to refer to both. In this paper, I use the term *methods* to refer to prototypical methods that are conceptualized by theorists, not those that are actualized by teachers in their classrooms.

The exact number of methods conceptualized by theorists is not clear. A book published in the mid-sixties, for instance, provides a list of fifteen 'most common' types of methods 'still in use in one form or another in various parts of the world' (Mackey 1965: 151). Two books published in the mid-eighties (Larsen-Freeman 1986 and Richards & Rodgers 1986) – the ones that are widely prescribed for methods classes in the United States – provide, between them, a list of eleven methods that are currently used. They are (in alphabetical order): Audiolingual Method, Communicative Methods, Community Language Learning, Direct Method, Grammar-Translation Method, Natural Approach, Oral Approach, Silent Way, Situational Language Teaching, Suggestopedia, and Total Physical Response.

Each established method is supposed to have a specified set of theoretical principles and a specific set of classroom practices. One might think, therefore, that the eleven methods listed above provide eleven different paths to language learning and teaching. That is not so. In fact, there is a considerable overlap in their theory and practice. As Wilga Rivers rightly points out, what appears to be a radically new method is more often than not a variant of existing methods presented with 'the fresh paint of a new terminology that camouflages their fundamental similarity' (1991: 283).

While theorists produced and promoted a succession of methods, teachers found it impossible to implement any of them as designed and delivered to them. In fact, even the authors of the two textbooks on methods widely used in the United States were uneasy about the efficacy of the methods they selected to include in their books, and wisely refrained from recommending any of them for adoption. 'Our goal,' Jack Richards and Ted Rodgers (1986: viii) told their readers, 'is to enable teachers to become better informed about the nature, strengths, and weaknesses of methods and approaches so they can better arrive at their own judgments and decisions.' Diane Larsen-Freeman (1986:1) went a step further and explicitly warned her readers that 'the inclusion of a method in this book should not be construed as an endorsement of that method. What *is* being recommended is that, in the interest of becoming informed about existing choices, you investigate each method' (emphasis as in original).

The disjunction between methods as conceptualized by theorists and methods as actualized by practitioners is the direct consequence of the inherent limitations of the concept of method itself. First and foremost, methods are founded on idealized concepts geared towards idealized contexts. Since language learning/teaching needs, wants and situations are unpredictably numerous, no idealized method can visualize all the variables in advance in order to provide situation-specific solutions that practising teachers sorely need to tackle the challenges they confront every day in their professional lives.

Secondly, as a predominantly top-down exercise, the conception and construction of method have been largely guided by a one-size-fits-all, cookie-cutter approach that assumes a generic clientèle with common goals. Preoccupied with their potential global reach, methods have lacked an essential local touch. Clearly, methods that are manufactured and marketed as usable in *all* learning/teaching contexts cannot be useful to *any* learning/teaching context.

Thirdly, not anchored in any specific learning/teaching context, and caught up in the whirlwind of fashion, methods tend to drift wildly from one theoretical extreme to the other. These extreme swings create conditions in which certain aspects of learning/teaching (such as grammar or meaning) get overly emphasized, while certain others are utterly ignored, depending on which way the wind blows.

Finally, the concept of method is too inadequate and too limited to satisfactorily explain the complexity of language teaching operations. Concerned primarily and narrowly with classroom instructional strategies, it ignores the fact that the success or failure of classroom instruction depends to a large extent on the unstated and unstable interaction of multiple factors such as teacher cognition, learner perception, societal needs, cultural contexts, political exigencies, economic imperatives and institutional constraints, all of which are inextricably interwoven.

The limitations of the concept of method gradually led to the realization that 'the term method is a label without substance' (Clarke 1983: 109), that it has 'diminished rather than enhanced our understanding of language teaching' (Pennycook 1989: 597), and that 'language teaching might be better understood and better executed if the concept of method were not to exist at all' (Jarvis 1991: 295). This realization is at once the result of and a reason for the emergence of what might be called antimethod sentiments.

Antimethod

Teachers and teacher educators have expressed their antipathy to method in different but related ways. Studies by Swaffar, Arens & Morgan (1982), Nunan (1987), Kumaravadivelu (1993/1996) and others clearly demonstrate that even as the methodological band played on, practising teachers were marching to a different drum. Collectively, these studies show that (a) teachers who are trained in and swear by a particular method do not conform or confine themselves to its theoretical principles and classroom procedures, (b) teachers who claim to follow the same method often use different classroom procedures, (c) teachers who claim to follow different methods often use the same classroom procedures, and (d) over time, teachers develop and follow a carefully delineated task-hierarchy, a weighted sequence of activities not necessarily associated with any established method.

Justifiable dissatisfaction with established methods inevitably and increasingly led practising teachers to rely to a great extent on their intuitive ability and experiential knowledge. As Henry Widdowson observes: 'It is quite common to hear teachers say that they do not subscribe to any particular approach or method in their teaching but are "eclectic". They thereby avoid commitment to any current fad that comes up on the whirligig of fashion.' (1990: 50) He further asserts that 'if by eclecticism is meant the random and expedient use of whatever technique comes most readily to hand, then it has no merit whatever.' (ibid) While there have been frequent calls for teachers to develop principled eclecticism based on their own understanding of the strengths and weaknesses of established methods, teacher education programmes seldom make any sustained or systematic effort to develop in prospective teachers the knowledge and skill necessary to be responsibly eclectic.

The difficulties faced by teachers in developing enlightened eclectic methods are not difficult to find. Stern pointed out some of them. 'The weakness of the eclectic position is that it offers no criteria according to which we can determine which is the best theory, nor does it provide any principles by which to include or exclude features which form part of existing theories or practices. The choice is left to the individual's intuitive judgment and is, therefore, too broad and too vague to be satisfactory as a theory in its own right.' (1992: 11) The net result is that practising teachers have neither the comfort of a context-sensitive professional theory that they can rely on nor the confidence of a fully developed personal theory that they can build on. Consequently, they find themselves straddling two methodological worlds: one that is imposed on them, and the other that is improvised by them.

Teachers' efforts to cope with the limitations of method are matched by teacher educators' attempts to develop images, options, scenarios, tasks or activities based on a fast-developing knowledge of the processes of second language acquisition and on a growing understanding of the dynamics of classroom learning/teaching. For instance, drawing 'from a wider range of methods – some old, some new, some widely used, some relatively unknown', Stevick (1982: 2) attempted to aid teachers in identifying and evaluating many of the alternatives that are available for their day-to-day work in the classroom. Looking at second language learning and teaching from a perspective in which proficiency is the organizing principle, Omaggio advocated a proficiency-oriented instruction that focuses on 'a hierarchy of priorities set by the instructor or the program planners rather than a "prepackaged" set of procedures to which everyone is expected to slavishly subscribe' (1986: 44). Di Pietro proposed strategic interaction with scenarios that motivate students 'to converse purposefully with each other by casting them in roles in episodes based on or taken from real life' (1987: 2).

Several other scholars tried to nudge the profession away from the concept of method. David Nunan sought to assign 'the search for the one right method to the dustbin' by helping teachers to 'develop, select, or adapt tasks which are appropriate in terms of goals, input, activities, roles and settings, and difficulty' (1989: 2). Dick Allwright propagated the concept of exploratory teaching that teachers can pursue in their own classroom settings (see, for instance, Allwright & Bailey 1991). Chiding the profession for its obsession with method, Stern proposed 'teaching strategies' based on intralingual-crosslingual, analytic-experiential, and explicit-implicit dimensions. His comprehensive and coherent approach to language teaching is derived from 'flexible sets of concepts which embody any useful lessons we can draw from the history of language teaching but which do not perpetuate the rigidities and dogmatic narrowness of the earlier methods concept' (1992: 278).

What have gradually emerged over the years, and in an accelerated way during the last decade, are critical thoughts that question the nature and scope of method, and creative ideas that redefine our understanding of method. Having witnessed how methods go through endless cycles of life, death and rebirth, we now seem to have reached a state of heightened awareness – an awareness that as long as we are caught up in the web of method, we will continue to get entangled in an unending search for an unavailable solution, an awareness that such a search drives us to continually recycle and repackage the same old ideas, and an awareness that nothing short of breaking the cycle can salvage the situation. Out of this awareness has emerged what I have called a 'postmethod condition' (Kumaravadivelu 1994).

Postmethod

In a nutshell, the postmethod condition signifies a search for an alternative *to* method rather than an alternative method. There may very well be several alternatives to method. I offer one such alternative in the form of what I have called a postmethod pedagogy (see Kumaravadivelu 2001 for more details). I visualize postmethod pedagogy as a three-dimensional system consisting of three parameters: particularity, practicality and possibility.

The parameter of particularity

The first parameter deals with the notion of particularity. It is based on the firm belief that all pedagogy, like all politics, is local. To ignore local exigencies is to ignore lived experiences. A language teaching programme, therefore, must be sensitive to a particular group of teachers teaching a particular group of learners pursuing a particular set of goals within a particular institutional context embedded in a particular sociocultural milieu. A pedagogy of particularity, then, is completely antithetical to the idea that there can be one set of learning and teaching goals realizable through one set of theoretical principles and classroom practices.

Any pedagogy that is not sensitive to the local individual, institutional, social and cultural contexts in which learning and teaching take place becomes irrelevant, and is doomed to failure because it is the critical awareness of local conditions that triggers the exploration and achievement of a pedagogy of particularity. This critical awareness starts with practising teachers, either individually or collectively, assessing local needs, observing their teaching acts, evaluating their outcomes, identifying problems, finding solutions, and trying them out to see once again what works and what doesn't. Such a continual cycle of observation, reflection and action is a prerequisite for the development of context-sensitive pedagogic knowledge. Since the particular is so deeply embedded in the practical, and cannot be achieved or understood without it, the parameter of particularity is intertwined with the parameter of practicality.

The parameter of practicality

The parameter of practicality refers not only to the practice of classroom teaching, but also to a much larger issue that directly impacts on classroom teaching, namely, the relationship between theory and practice. There is at present an unfortunate and unproductive division of labour between the theorist and the teacher: the theorist is supposed to produce knowledge; the teacher is supposed to consume knowledge. Teachers are seldom enabled to conceive and construct their own personal theories; instead, they are often encouraged to understand and apply professional theories produced by others.

What the parameter of practicality aims for is a personal theory of practice generated by the teacher. This assertion is premised on a rather simple and straightforward proposition: no theory of practice can be useful and usable unless it is generated *through* practice. A logical corollary is that it is the practising teacher who, given adequate tools for exploration, is best suited to produce such a practical theory.

A theory of practice develops, as van Manen (1977) observes, when there is a union of action and thought, when there is action in thought and thought in action. Based on their action and thought, teachers develop an unexplained and sometimes unexplainable awareness of what constitutes good teaching. Such an awareness has been given different labels by different scholars. Van Manen calls it 'sense-making'. Prabhu (1990) calls it a 'sense of plausibility'. Freeman (1996) calls it a 'conception of practice'. Hargreaves (1994) calls it 'the ethic of practicality'. They all refer to the same thing, namely, a teacher's powerful sense of what works and what doesn't.

A teacher's personal theory of practice does not involve any grand theorizing, nor does it involve complicated experimental studies, for which teachers have neither the time nor the energy. Rather, it involves keeping one's eyes and ears and mind open in the classroom to see what works and what doesn't, with what group(s) of learners, for what reasons, and assessing what changes are necessary to make instruction achieve its desired goals.

A personal theory of practice is created and recreated when teachers extend their intuitive ability and conduct a more structured and more goal-oriented exploratory research based on the parameters of particularity, practicality and possibility. It is doable if it is not separated from and is fully integrated with day-to-day teaching and learning. It involves continual reflection and action. It is formed and re-formed not only by the pedagogic factors governing the microcosm of the classroom, but also by the socio-political forces emanating from outside. In this sense, the parameter of practicality metamorphoses into the parameter of possibility.

The parameter of possibility

The parameter of possibility is derived mainly from the critical pedagogy advocated by Paulo Freire and his followers. Critical pedagogists such as Simon (1988) and Giroux (1988) take the position that pedagogy, any pedagogy, is implicated in relations of power and dominance, and is implemented to create and sustain social inequalities. For them, educational institutions are not simply instructional sites; they are, in fact, arenas where various ideological, cultural, and social forms collide with each other.

Classroom reality is socially constructed and historically determined. What is therefore required to counter the social and historical forces that strive to maintain the status quo is a pedagogy of possibility that empowers participants to critically appropriate forms of knowledge outside their immediate experience. Such a pedagogy of possibility would take seriously the social and historical conditions which create the cultural forms and interested knowledge that give meaning to the lives of teachers and learners.

The lived experiences participants bring to the classroom setting are shaped not just by the learning/teaching episodes they have encountered in the past, but also by a broader social, economic and political environment in which they grow up. These experiences have the potential to alter classroom practices in ways unintended and unexpected by policy planners or curriculum designers or textbook producers. We often hear stories about how L2 learners, motivated by their own cultural and historical backgrounds, appropriate the English language and use it in their own terms according to their own aspirations, needs and values.

In the process of sensitizing itself to the prevailing sociopolitical reality, the parameter of possibility is also concerned with individual identity. More than any other educational enterprise, language education provides its participants with challenges and opportunities for a continual quest for subjectivity and self-identity. As Weedon points out, 'language is the place where actual and possible forms of social organization and their likely social and political consequences are defined and contested. Yet it is also the place where our sense of ourselves, our subjectivity, is constructed.' (1987: 21)

This quest for self-identity assumes greater importance these days because of fast-emerging economic and cultural globalization. As a recent United Nations Report points out, 'Contacts between people and their cultures – their ideas, their values, their way of life – have been growing and deepening in unprecedented ways' (United Nations, 1999: 30). And English, being the global language, carries with it and transmits cultural meanings that some people consider a threat to local cultural identity. L2 teachers, therefore, cannot afford to ignore the global sociocultural reality that influences identity formation in the classroom, nor can they afford to separate the linguistic needs of learners from their social needs. In other words, they cannot hope to fully satisfy their pedagogic obligations without at the same time satisfying their social obligations.

To sum up, I have suggested that one way of conceptualizing a postmethod pedagogy is to look at it in terms of parameters of particularity, practicality and possibility. The boundaries of the particular, the practical and the possible are inevitably blurred. They interweave and interact with each other in a synergistic relationship where the whole is greater than the sum of its parts. How do we translate the essentials of a postmethod pedagogy into a workable proposition in a classroom context? For that, I believe we need a coherent pedagogic framework. I present below one such framework – a macrostrategic framework.

Macrostrategic framework

The macrostrategic framework for language teaching consists of macrostrategies and microstrategies. I define macrostrategies as guiding principles derived from theoretical, empirical and experiential insights related to EFL learning and teaching. A macrostrategy is thus a general plan, a broad guideline on the basis of which teachers will be able to generate their own situation-specific, needs-based microstrategies or classroom techniques. In other words, macrostrategies are made operational in the classroom through microstrategies.

Based on my own experiential knowledge as a teacher and teacher educator, and on my understanding of theoretical and empirical research in the field of English as a second language and foreign language learning and teaching, I have derived ten macrostrategies. I have framed them in operational terms to denote their operational character. The choice of action verbs over static nouns to frame these macrostrategies should not be misunderstood as an attempt to convey any prescriptive quality. Let me briefly outline each of these ten macrostrategies:

1 **Maximize learning opportunities**: This is about teaching as a process of creating and utilizing learning opportunities, a process in which teachers strike a balance between their role as managers of teaching and their role as mediators of learning.

2 **Minimize perceptual mismatches**: This is about recognizing potential mismatches between teacher intention and learner interpretation, and what to do about them.

3 **Facilitate negotiated interaction**: This is about ensuring meaningful learner–learner and learner–teacher classroom interaction in which learners are entitled and encouraged to initiate topic and talk, not just react and respond.

4 **Promote learner autonomy**: This is about helping learners learn to learn, and also learn to liberate; how to equip them with the means necessary to self-direct and self-monitor their own learning.

5 **Foster language awareness**: This is about creating general language awareness as well as critical language awareness; how to draw learners' attention to the formal and functional properties of the language as well as how to make them aware of the insidious power of language.

6 **Activate intuitive heuristics**: This is about providing rich textual data so that learners can infer and internalize the underlying rules governing grammatical usage and communicative use; how to help learners in the process of their grammar construction.

7 **Contextualize linguistic input**: This is about how language usage and use are shaped by linguistic, social and cultural contexts.

8 **Integrate language skills**: This is about the need to holistically integrate language skills traditionally separated and sequenced as listening, speaking, reading and writing.

9 **Ensure social relevance**: This is about the need for teachers to be sensitive to the societal, political, economic, and educational environment in which EFL learning and teaching take place.

10 **Raise cultural consciousness**: This emphasizes the need to treat learners as cultural informants so that they are encouraged to engage in a process of classroom participation that puts a premium on their power/knowledge, on their subjectivity and identity.

These macrostrategies are general operating principles. What shape and form each will take will vary from country to country, from context to context, and in fact, from teacher to teacher. Teachers can use the macrostrategic framework to begin to construct their own theory of practice. They can also use it to self-observe, self-analyze and self-evaluate their own teaching acts (see Kumaravadivelu 2002 for details).

In closing

Pointing out the limited and limiting nature of the concept of method, and the dissatisfaction it has created among teachers and teacher educators, I have argued for the development of a postmethod pedagogy founded on the parameters of particularity, practicality and possibility. Consistent with that conceptual foundation, I have suggested a macrostrategic framework derived from theoretical, empirical and experiential knowledge.

The macrostrategic framework has the potential to help teachers develop the knowledge, skill, attitudes and autonomy necessary to devise for themselves a systematic, coherent and relevant personal theory of practice that is grounded in the parameters of particularity, practicality and possibility. While the purpose of such a framework is to help teachers become autonomous decision-makers, it should, without denying the value of individual autonomy, provide a set of operating principles so that their teaching acts may come about in a principled fashion.

References

Allwright, R. L. & K. M. Bailey (1991) *Focus on the Language Classroom*. Cambridge: Cambridge University Press.

Clarke, M. A. (1983) The scope of approach, the importance of method, and the nature of technique. In Alatis, J. E., H. Stern & P. Strevens (Eds.), *Georgetown University Round Table on Languages and Linguistics 1983: Applied Linguistics and the Preparation of Second Language Teachers* (pp. 106–115). Washington, D.C.: Georgetown University.

Di Pietro, R. (1987) *Strategic interaction: learning languages through scenarios*. Cambridge: Cambridge University Press.

Freeman, D. (1996) Redefining the relationship between research and what teachers know. In Bailey, K. & D. Nunan, (Eds.) *Voices from the Language Classroom* (pp. 88–115). Cambridge: Cambridge University Press.

Giroux, H. A. (1988) *Schooling and the struggle for public life: Critical pedagogy in the modern age*. Minneapolis: University of Minnesota Press.

Hargreaves, A. (1994) *Changing Teachers; Changing Times*. NY: Teachers College Press.

Jarvis, G. A. (1991) Research on Teaching Methodology: Its evolution and prospects. In Freed, B.

(Ed.) *Foreign Language Acquisition Research and the Classroom* (pp. 295–306). MA: D. C. Heath and Company.

Kumaravadivelu, B. (1993/1996). Maximizing learning potential in the communicative classroom. In *ELT Journal* 47:1:12–21. Reprinted in Hedge, T. & N. Whitney (Eds.) *Power, Pedagogy and Practice* (pp. 241–353). 1996. Oxford: Oxford University Press.

Kumaravadivelu, B. (1994) The postmethod condition: (E)merging strategies for second/foreign language teaching. In *TESOL Quarterly,* 28:1:27–48.

Kumaravadivelu, B. (2001) Toward a postmethod pedagogy. In *TESOL Quarterly*, 35: 37–560.

Kumaravadivelu, B. (2002) *Macrostrategies for Language Teaching.* New Haven, CT.: Yale University Press.

Larsen-Freeman, D. (1986) *Techniques and Principles in Language Teaching.* Oxford: Oxford University Press.

Mackey, W. F. (1965) *Language Teaching Analysis.* Bloomington: Indiana University Press.

Nunan, D. (1987) Communicative language teaching: making it work. In *ELT Journal* 41/2:136–145.

Nunan, D. (1989) *Understanding Language Classrooms: A Guide for Teacher-initiated Action.* New York: Prentice Hall.

Omaggio, A. C. (1986) *Teaching Language in Context.* Boston, MA: Heinle & Heinle.

Pennycook, A. (1989) The concept of method, interested knowledge, and the politics of language teaching. In *TESOL Quarterly*, 23:4:589–618.

Prabhu, N. S. (1990) There is no best method – why? In *TESOL Quarterly* 24:2:161–176.

Richards, J. C. & T. Rodgers (1986) *Approaches and Methods in Language Teaching.* Cambridge: Cambridge University Press.

Rivers, W. M. (1991) Psychological validation of methodological approaches and foreign language classroom practices. In Barbara Freed (Ed.) *Foreign Language Acquisition Research and the Classroom* (pp. 283–294). Mass.: D. C. Heath & Co.

Simon, R. (1988) For a pedagogy of possibility. In J. Smyth (Ed.), *The Critical Pedagogy Networker*, 1:1:1–4. Victoria, Australia: Deakin University Press.

Stern, H. H. (1992) *Issues and Options in Language Teaching.* Oxford: Oxford University Press.

Stevick, E. W. (1982) *Teaching and Learning Languages.* Cambridge: Cambridge University Press.

Swaffar, J., Arens, K., & Morgan, M. (1982) Teacher classroom practices: redefining method as task hierarchy. In *Modern Language Journal*, 66, 24–33.

United Nations Human Development Report 1999 (1999) New York: UNDP & Oxford University Press.

van Manen, M. (1977) Linking ways of knowing with ways of being practical. In *Curriculum Inquiry* 6:3:205–228.

Weedon, C. (1987) *Feminist practice and poststructuralist theory.* London: Blackwell.

Widdowson, H. (1990) *Aspects of Language Teaching.* Oxford: Oxford University Press.

1.2 Workshop: Fostering language awareness

B. Kumaravadivelu

Towards the end of my Plenary talk on Method, Antimethod, Postmethod, I presented the outline of a macrostrategic framework consisting of ten macrostrategies. I defined macrostrategies as guiding principles derived from historical, theoretical, empirical and experiential insights related to second/foreign language learning and teaching. Macrostrategies offer operating principles based on which teachers will be able to generate their own situation-specific, needs-based microstrategies or classroom techniques.

The workshop was aimed at providing sample microstrategies for one macrostrategy, namely, fostering language awareness. I began the workshop by suggesting that language awareness can be discussed under two broad categories: (a) general language awareness that deals with the awareness of linguistic factors governing language usage; and (b) critical language awareness that deals with the awareness of social, political and historical factors governing language use. British as well as American scholars have sought to promote general language awareness among schoolchildren by bridging the gap between primary and secondary school language-related work, by promoting holistic language experience that integrates listening, speaking, reading and writing, and by introducing language activities across the curriculum through tasks relevant to learners and their daily lives. I also pointed out that focusing narrowly on the logic of linguistic systems and skills, general language awareness has ignored the broader role language plays in shaping and reshaping human lives.

Critical language awareness emphasizes, in addition to linguistic usage, the socio-political nature of language use. Language is linked to power; therefore, a critical awareness of the word is essential to develop a critical awareness of the world. To help learners understand how power is produced, maintained and resisted through language, teachers should select appropriate materials that sensitize learners to subtle meanings, concealed assumptions and hidden attitudes; use class activity to incorporate open-ended questions; recognize a variety of viewpoints; deal with different linguistic and cultural perspectives; and design and use supplementary materials relevant to the needs and wants of a given group of learners.

To illustrate how critical language awareness can be fostered in the L2 classroom, I presented the outlines of two microstrategies, the first on The Language of Doublespeak, and the second on The Language of Political Apologies. I stopped at crucial points to ask the workshop participants how they would proceed with the activities.

Responding to my questions, the participants, about 100 in total, suggested various ways in which the textual prompts I presented can be used to promote critical language awareness in class. I then shared my own prepared set of strategies, which are, for the most part, very similar to the ones the participants came up with.

I present below the outlines of one of the microstrategies I presented:

Macrostrategy The language of political apologies

Objective To promote critical language awareness by helping learners explore the language of political apologies between nations, or between various groups of people within a nation.

Materials News items from the archives of online newspapers, collected from the Internet.

1 Recently, we have been witnessing a global phenomenon: official apologies emanating from political as well as religious leaders of the world for real or perceived human rights abuses of the past. Examine the archives of the online edition of a national newspaper (or a news magazine) of your choice. Go to any search engines on the Internet (such as Yahoo, Google). Look for information on recent political apologies.

2 Your research will reveal several political apologies of sensitive nature: (a) the Pope apologizing to the Jews for the Vatican's indifference during the Holocaust; (b) the United States apologizing to Japanese-Americans for their internment during the Second World War; (c) Japan apologizing to some of its Asian neighbors for treating enemy women as 'comfort women', and so on.

3 Select one case that you came up with in your archival research. Then write an outline of a classroom activity – to make your learners aware of the complex factors (e.g. historical, political, national, cultural, linguistic) involved in political apologies, keeping in mind the proficiency level of your students.

4 Think about the best way of carrying out the classroom activity – through group work? Pair work? Role play? How to steer class discussion to achieve the major objective of creating critical language awareness?

5 If it is difficult to do archival research on the Internet, focus on current newspapers or news magazines and select stories of political apologies that are linguistically and conceptually appropriate to your class. Here's one such story; you may find others.

> In April 2001, a Chinese interceptor plane and a U.S. intelligence plane collided off China's southern coast, killing the Chinese pilot, Wang Wei. The American spy plane, with its 24-member crew, made a safe emergency landing on Hainan island without formal approval from the Chinese air traffic control. The Chinese government demanded a formal apology from the American government. After prolonged negotiation between the two countries, the matter was resolved. Here's how the online edition of *The Washington Post* reported the story. (www.washingtonpost.com/wp-dyn/articles/A6425-2001Apr11.html). Only one-third of the story is reproduced below, unedited.

Resolving Crisis Was a Matter of Interpretation
by John Pomfret
Washington Post Foreign Service
Thursday, April 12, 2001; Page A01

BEIJING, April 11 – In the end, it was a matter of what the United States chose to say and what China chose to hear.

The letter that U.S. Ambassador Joseph W. Prueher handed to Chinese Foreign Minister Tang Jiaxuan today asked Tang to 'convey to the Chinese people and to the family of pilot Wang Wei that we are very sorry for their loss.' And it said, 'We are very sorry the entering of China's airspace and the landing did not have verbal clearance.'

The word 'apology' did not appear in the English-language document handed to Tang. But in announcing the U.S. move and describing the letter to the Chinese people, China chose to translate the double 'very sorry' as 'shenbiao qianyi', which means 'a deep expression of apology or regret'.

And the deal was done, with both sides proclaiming they got what they wanted.

'In Chinese, you don't use that phrase unless you're admitting you're wrong and accepting responsibility,' said Mei Renyi, director of the American Studies Center at Beijing Foreign Studies University. 'If they're translating it that way, especially in the context of a formal letter, it means the U.S. is admitting it was wrong.'

But a translation into Chinese released by the U.S. Embassy used other language. For 'very sorry' it used the Chinese words 'feichang wanxi', which linguists described as an expression of great sympathy but not an apology. It also used 'feichang baoqian', or 'extremely sorry' ...

6 Plan how to start the activity in class. Would it be helpful to make a connection between personal apologies and political apologies? For instance, ask your learners to imagine day-to-day situations where people normally tender an apology, preferably one in a formal context and another in an informal context. (If your learners fail to come up with any, you could suggest a couple of scenarios; e.g. a job-seeker apologizing to a potential employer for being late for a job interview, or a teenager apologizing to parents for returning home very late after a date on a Saturday night).
7 Plan how you will conduct your classroom activity in terms of group work, whole-class discussion, etc.
8 Plan how you can explicitly draw your learners' attention to how English usage varies between formal and informal contexts for apologizing, or how the realization of apology as a speech act varies in first and second language speech communities.
9 Design an appropriate take-home writing assignment for your students on any aspect of political apologies.
10 Finally, reflect on the desirability or the difficulty of discussing topics such as political apology in your class. What difficulties do you anticipate if you do decide to take up such topics for discussion in class? Later, compare your anticipated difficulties with how the students actually reacted to the classroom activity.

The workshop generated a lively discussion among the participants. They generally agreed on the need to foster critical language awareness in the classroom. They also recognized the need to go beyond the limited opportunity provided by commercially produced textbooks in fostering critical language awareness. They felt that, in these days of cultural globalization and information technology, sources such as the Internet offer unlimited possibilities for practising teachers to tap to design microstrategies that are highly relevant to the needs and wants and situations of a given group of learners.

2 LOOKING AT LANGUAGE

2.1 Plenary: Understanding language[1]

Diane Larsen-Freeman *University of Michigan, USA*

1 What is language?

What is language? You may or may not have thought about this question before. Nevertheless, I think that it is an important question for you to consider because your answer to this question will inform your beliefs about language teaching and learning, and what you do in the classroom as you teach language. As Becker (1983) put it, 'Our "picture" of language is the single most important factor ... in determining the way we choose to teach one.'

Now you may feel that Becker has overstated the case, as clearly one's students, their reasons for learning, and contextual factors will all influence the way we teach. Nevertheless, it is well known that the way we conceptualize our subject matter does shape the way we approach its teaching.

Here is a list of other language educators' answers to the question about the nature of language that I have culled from the literature of the past 100 years or so and then paraphrased.

1 Language is a means of cultural transmission.
2 Language is what people use to talk about the things that are important to them, for example, occurrences in their everyday lives.
3 Language is a set of sound (or sign in the case of sign language), word and structure patterns that express meaning.
4 Language is a set of rules through which humans can create and understand novel utterances, ones that they have never before articulated or encountered.
5 Language is a means of interaction between and among people.
6 Language is the means for doing something – accomplishing some purpose such as agreeing on a common plan of action for handling a conflict.
7 Language is a vehicle for communicating meaning and messages.
8 Language is an instrument of power (those that know a language are empowered in a way that those who do not are not).
9 Language is a medium through which one can learn other things.
10 Language is holistic and is therefore best understood as it is manifest in discourse or whole texts.

Corresponding syllabus units

It should be clear why I have chosen to begin by asking you to define language for yourself. Despite some overlap among the ten definitions, each presents a view of language that may be realized in a language classroom in quite distinct ways. For instance, depending upon to which view of language you subscribe, you may choose different elements or aspects of language to foreground. To illustrate this point more concretely, the following are examples of syllabus units corresponding to the first three definitions:

1 cultural transmission: works of literature, poetry, history, and the grammar structures and vocabulary words that constitute them
2 everyday life: talking about family, daily routines, situations (e.g. shopping, going to the post office)
3 patterns: fixed and semi-fixed lexicogrammatical patterns and sequences such as 'How are you?' 'I am fine.' 'Thank you.' 'And you?' and sound contrasts, intonation, rhythm, stress patterns that result in differences in meaning

Linking definitions of language and theories of learning

Not only may your definition of language influence your decisions about syllabus units, but it may also shape your view of learning. Although the link between a particular view of language and a particular theory of learning is not inevitable, some theories of learning fit more naturally with certain definitions of language than others. For example, in the past, those who have seen language as a set of sound/sign, word and structure patterns (definition #3) were working in a period of time when a *behaviorist* theory of learning was prominent in psychology. Consistent with such a theory is the habit formation view of language learning, in which it is seen to be the responsibility of the teacher to help students overcome the pattern habits of the native language and replace them with the habits of the second language. In contrast, those who have seen language as a set of rules (definition #4) might embrace a *cognitivist* explanation for learning and expect students to formulate and test hypotheses in order for students to discover and internalize the rules of the language they are learning. To cite a final example, those who define language as a means of interaction among people (definition #5) are likely to subscribe to an *interactionist* view of the learning process – one that calls for students to interact with each other, however imperfectly, right from the inception of instruction, believing that such interaction facilitates the language acquisition process.

Associating teaching practices with definitions of language

In addition to foregrounding certain syllabus units and privileging certain theories of language learning, your definition of language might also determine your choice of teaching practices. Indeed, each of the ten definitions of language above could easily be associated with common language teaching practices. To cite just one example from three of them:

6 means of doing something: communicative activities and tasks, e.g. asking for and giving directions, surveying class preferences
7 vehicle for communicating meaning: Total Physical Response (TPR) activities, in which the meaning of lexical items and messages is made clear through actions
8 instrument of power: problem-posing activities, in which students discuss solutions to their own real-world problems

Some caveats

So far I have suggested that your definition of language has a powerful influence that extends beyond a conception of language and could impact on your view of its acquisition and your teaching practice. However, before proceeding any further, a number of caveats are in order. First of all, many people's definitions of language are broader than any one of the ten on the list, overlapping with some of them, but not quite lining up with any one in particular. Perhaps this is the case with yours. Because language is as complex as it is, each of the ten definitions is not exclusive.

Second, the coherence among language, learning and teaching beliefs is often more theoretical than actual. This is because there are many other important considerations in teaching. For instance, teachers have to take into account who their students are and why they are studying the language. An assessment of students' language needs should inform the choice of syllabus units and teaching practices. We are after all, teaching students, not just teaching language.

Further, often there are contextual factors, such as having to prepare students for particular standardized examinations or having to adopt prescribed textbooks, which constrain teachers' freedom to define their subject matter. In other words, the subject matter is defined for teachers by materials/test developers. This is why I have been careful to use words such as 'may', 'might,' 'could' and 'likely' when I have been discussing the links among one's 'picture' of language, theory of learning, and teaching practice. In language teaching, everything is connected to everything else. It is difficult to conceive of language separately from who one is as a teacher, who one's students and colleagues are, what the demands of the curriculum are, etc. Indeed, at the level of practice, most teachers are less likely to adhere to a narrow view of language, learning or teaching. Most teachers and/or the texts that they use are more eclectic, interweaving a variety of syllabus and activity types into lessons.

Nevertheless, I would still maintain that a language teacher's conception of language is not inconsequential in influencing the teacher's practice. Therefore I want to offer yet another conception of language – one that I believe is on the edge of our awareness, but that promises to have a major impact on our conception of our subject matter. I am speaking of a conception of language that is much more dynamic in nature than any of the ten in the list that I presented earlier.

2 The 'inert knowledge problem'

Elman has written about dynamic systems theory:

> Periodically in science there arrive on the scene what appear to be dramatically new theoretical frameworks ... Characteristic of such changes in perspective is the recasting of old problems in new terms. By altering the conceptual vocabulary we use to think about problems, we may discover solutions which were obscured by prior ways of thinking about things.

I submit to you today that thinking about language as a dynamic system has the potential to help us with a new way to address an old problem, most aptly termed the 'inert knowledge problem' by the philosopher, A. N. Whitehead. The inert knowledge problem, as the name suggests, refers to the commonly observed lack of facility students have for using outside of the classroom what they have learned inside it – or, indeed, even in a different part of the lesson – for instance, making use of some grammar rule that they appeared to have mastered in the grammar portion of a lesson, but which is nowhere to be seen in some subsequent communicative activity which entails its use. I expect that this problem afflicts many who study languages. I also expect that it is what causes those who have the option to do so to discontinue their study of language because they feel that they cannot do much of anything with what they have learned. Therefore, in my estimation, it is indeed a problem worthy of our attention and one that might be at least ameliorated if language were to be treated more dynamically.

3 Language as a dynamic system

There are several ways in which we might think of language as dynamic. One is that a language changes over time. It is common knowledge that the English of today is different from the English of several centuries ago – even though it is undeniably the same language. For example, in an earlier state of the English language, the second person pronoun 'you' was defined by its opposition to 'ye' ('ye' a subject pronoun and 'you' an object pronoun) and to 'thee' and 'thou' ('thee' and 'thou' being singular forms and 'ye' and 'you' plural forms). Later, 'you' became a respectful way of addressing one person, like the modern French 'vous' or the Spanish 'usted'. Today, in modern English, 'you' refers to both one person and to many, and can function as either the subject or object in a sentence, not especially connoting respect. Languages are thus dynamic. Their *synchronic* state at one point in time is distinct from their *diachronic* development over time.

While we might call such evolutionary changes 'over time dynamism', the second well-known way that languages can be said to be dynamic can be referred to as 'online dynamism'. Helpful in understanding the second type of dynamism is to think of the contrast between product and process. It is true that language can be described as an aggregation of static units or products, parts of speech such as nouns and verbs, for example, but their use in actual speech involves an active process. Language users must constantly be scanning the environment, observing their interlocutors and interpreting what they are hearing/seeing, in order to make decisions about how to respond in accurate, meaningful and appropriate ways, and then carry out their decisions 'online', i.e. they must then somehow activate what they have decided upon. This clearly entails a dynamic process.

Thus far, I have spoken of two notions of the term dynamic: change over time and language use online. There is yet a third type of dynamism that it would be worth our while to consider and that is the dynamic connection that is made at the intersection of the first two types. After all, when we say that language changes over time, what do we really mean? Language does not change of its own accord. On the other hand, changes in a language are not usually the product of wilful attempts on the part of users to alter the code. If that were possible, we could all pledge today to refrain from using the present perfect and thus spare many language teachers and students from agonizing over the choice between using it or the past simple. This is not to deny that a user may from time to time deliberately strive to create linguistic innovations such as I have done by coining the term 'grammaring' to represent the ability to use grammatical structures accurately, meaningfully and appropriately (Larsen-Freeman 1991; see also Thornbury 2001). The point is that individuals may not intentionally seek to change language, but they do so by their day-to-day interactions in using it. Linguists refer to this as the Labov principle. Thus, the behavior of the system as a whole is the result of the aggregate of local interactions. I will refer to this third type of dynamism as organic dynamism.

Organic dynamism makes no distinction between current individual use of language (online dynamism) and its evolutionary change (over time dynamism) – they simply occur at different levels of scale. As I am speaking today and you are listening, we are changing English. At the level of the individual, this also takes place. As Karl Diller (1995: 116) put it, 'The act of using the language meaningfully has a way of changing the grammar in the user.'

In sum, it is important to recognize that while freezing and homogenizing language, as linguists do in order to describe a given language, has its theoretical/methodological advantages and its adherents, it also has its liabilities and its critics. By hypostasizing language for the purpose of studying its systematicity, we are in danger of conceptualizing language as an idealized, objectified, atemporal 'thing'. In order to know it, we feel we have to describe it in terms of its parts. The result is that we come to think of language in a mechanistic fashion.

While we have to be careful not to ascribe to a code a vitality of its own, since it is the people who use it who make it 'come alive', it is nevertheless attractive to think of language as a natural phenomenon, a dynamic organism. For instance, I was very moved the day that I realized that the structure of language and the structure of a natural product such as a leaf both were fractal – a very common naturally-occurring geometric pattern in nature (Larsen-Freeman 1997).[2]

I acknowledge that language can be seen both as a collection of products and as a process. It possesses both the flexibility to allow for the creation of new meanings and pragmatic uses, and the stability to facilitate mutual intelligibility and learnability. However, since the product view has dominated in recent times, today I have decided to emphasize the process view. Besides, I believe that 'organism' is a better general metaphor of developing interaction among humans. As Rutherford (1987: 37) put it so well: 'Machines are constructed, whereas organisms grow. Machines have precision; organisms have plasticity. Machines have linear connections; organisms have cyclical interconnections. And, perhaps most important of all, machines are sterile, whereas organisms are fecund.'[3]

4 Acquiring language as a dynamic system

Language as dynamic system conjures up biological/ecological associations for me. Naturally-occurring dynamic systems are said to be emergent. Emergence refers to the fact that such systems exhibit patterns that are not due to any domain-specific innate capacity nor are they *a priori* predictable or obvious from any input. Neither are the patterns the creation of some central executive who oversees their construction. Emergentism provides accounts in which structures emerge as the best solution to some 'problem'.

Honeycombs, for instance, are hexagonal in shape because that is the stable solution to the problem of packing relatively uniformly-sized balls of honey together. The shape of a honeycomb does not derive from properties of the wax, of the honey, or from the packing behavior of bees (Bates and Goodman 1999: 32). A similar argument has been made to explain the emergence of grammars, which represent the class of possible solutions to the problem of how to map a rich set of meanings onto a limited speech channel, heavily constrained by the limits of memory, perception and motor planning (Bates and

MacWhinney 1989). Those that subscribe to an emergentist view of language acquisition might say that 'the complexity of a solution emerges from the interaction of problem and solver'. The fact that the number of people queueing up in supermarket checkout lines stays roughly the same is an example of an emergent solution (MacWhinney 1999: ix).

Thus, the emergentist perspective leads to a very different view of language from language as a system of rules that generates a set of sentences in that language. It follows then that the language acquisition process is conceived differently as well. As Allen and Seidenberg (1999: 119–121) explain, from an emergentist point of view, children learning their native language are not attempting to identify rules in the language to which they are exposed. Instead, what children are engaged in is learning to use a language. In the course of mastering this task, they develop various types of knowledge representations that allow communication to proceed. The representations emerge as a function of the interplay among several factors, including the physical components of the human brain that are active during language processing, the tasks that such components are engaged in, and the characteristics of the language signals to which they are exposed through interaction with other members of the speech community.

But, how does such a view address Plato's problem? In other words, how does it account for output that is more complex than input? Mohanan (1992) answers with *morphogenesis*, which in this context refers to the process by which humans generate patterns. As Mohanan (1992: 653–654) puts it, 'Suppose we free ourselves from the idea that [first] language development is the deduction of the adult grammar from the input data, and think of it as the formation of patterns triggered by the data.'[4] In other words, rather than viewing grammar development as a process of discovery and adoption of the grammar of the community, which is governed by deductive and inductive operations, it is suggested that language development involves the creation of grammar, which then, as speakers communicate with each other, adapts itself to the overt patterns of the grammars of other individuals in the community. Such a perspective has been brought to bear on issues of second language acquisition as well as first (Larsen-Freeman 1997).

5 View of practice

Finally, then, what would conceiving of language as a dynamic system look like in practice? Another way of asking this question is to ask: How do you get students aboard a train that is moving and has already left the station?

While I confess to not having worked out all the details of my answer to this question, and I often think that it is easier to say what it is not than to say what it is (and I have no grand textbook scheme up my sleeve), I will offer you a few thoughts about how this new conception of language might influence practice. However, I have no monopoly on the crystal ball, and I invite you to draw your own implications – let the images play in your mind.

Both morphogenesis and emergentism present us with radical, but to my way of thinking, intriguing alternatives to the way that certain language teaching practices have recently been construed. For instance, at a recent TESOL Convention panel, I pointed to the absence of a theoretically-motivated developmental continuum for activities that involve language learners in meaningful use of language – not mechanical practice.[5] The alternative views that I have been discussing suggest that output production and meaningful use of language contribute to the creation of new knowledge, not just the rehearsal of previously-learned material, and account for the acquisition of language as different from the acquisition and application of rules.

Suppose we abandon the metaphor of the language learner as a scientist or a data-processing serial computer, and view language development as being analogous to the growth of form in a growing plant. What sort of teaching practice would this view encourage? I think a helpful answer to this question lies in Gleick's remark concerning dynamic systems (1987: 24): 'The act of playing the game has a way of changing the rules.' Clearly, this underscores the importance of learners having opportunities for use. In other words, real-time performance or practice is simultaneous with changes in underlying competence. It is not that we learn some rule or something about language and then we practise it. It is not a sequential process. From this perspective, through language use, language changes; through language use, language is acquired. Use, change and acquisition are all instances of the same underlying dynamic process. So it is not just that performance is made fluent through practice; the learner's internal system is *created* as a result of it.

Abundant use of linguistic forms (be they grammatical structures, formulas, lexical items, exponents of functions, Goldbergian constructions[6], etc.) is called for, then, but meaningful use – it is at the point of engagement when most learning is likely to take place. Further, the practice must contribute to building understanding. Such understanding may not be best served by giving students rules. Rules have traditionally served the learning of language by capturing generalizations about morphosyntactic regularities in a language. Rules also allow materials developers to work with 'right-sized' chunks of language, to help students deal in an orderly and systematic way with the grammar of the target language. They provide a modicum of security to language learners – they give them something to hold onto. Finally, they vest a certain amount of authority in the source of rules as well, the teacher.

However, there is also a cost to teaching language through rules. Rules are static descriptions of, or prescriptions about, the language. They encourage a conformity approach to language teaching. However, I have argued that language is anything but static. We can find support for this point in the fact that generalizations that rules attempt to capture are never broad enough to prevent exceptions. These are not necessarily due to the fact that the rules are poorly formulated, but rather (as we have seen) that grammar is flexible, allowing for the expression of new meanings – and we humans are meaning-making beings. Our students do need to understand the internal logic of English in order to be free to convey new meanings in accurate and appropriate ways themselves, but this capacity may be better built through understanding meaning-based reasons rather than simply form-based rules (Larsen-Freeman 2000a).

If the units of language are not fixed, but dynamic, they are subject to creative extension and reshaping with use. The linguistic forms would need to be grounded in discourse, because it is in discourse that the dynamism is most apparent. Just as an eddy only shows up in a moving stream of water, so many patterns in language are only apparent in the flow of discourse. For example, the dynamic patterning of *would* and *used to* or the chaining of given and new information in sentences that constitute a paragraph in order to produce coherent Z-shaped discourse patterns. And the only way to learn about the process of making pragmatic choices is by examining texts, the coherent product of discourse process.

Above all, the view of dynamic language promotes a *learning-centered* view. It recognizes that teaching does not cause learning, but rather is responsive to it, in proleptic fashion. It requires the teacher and the students to achieve a degree of intersubjectivity, which makes it possible for the teacher to guide the student, and for the student to be guided through the process of completing a task.

Lest I be guilty of committing a fallacy for which I have been unhappy with others, let me hasten to add that we should not be lured into the trap of believing that what works well in natural environments is what should be adhered to in the classroom. I have referred to this as 'the reflex fallacy' (Larsen-Freeman 1995), meaning that we should not automatically assume that it is our job to recreate within our classrooms the natural conditions of acquisition present in the external environment. What we want to do as language educators, it seems to me, is to improve upon natural acquisition, not emulate it. We do want our teaching to harmonize with our students' natural tendencies, but we want our teaching to accelerate the actual rate of acquisition beyond what students could achieve on their own.

As such, anyone (present company excluded, of course) who says, 'Don't do this and do only that' should be suspect. We know teaching is a contingent act that takes place in a complex social environment. Its practice does not lend itself to quick fixes or recipes. For this reason, teachers themselves need to cultivate attitudes of inquiry – to be fascinated with language and their students' learning of it (Larsen-Freeman 2000b). For the continuous stepping back, observing and responding humbly and respectfully in the service of one's students' learning helps to keep the dynamic language train on track.

References

Allen, J. & M. Seidenberg (1999) The emergence of grammaticality in connectionist networks. In MacWhinney, B. (Ed.) *The emergence of language* (pp. 115–151). Mahwah, NJ: Lawrence Erlbaum Associates, Publishers.

Bates, E. & J. Goodman (1999) On the emergence of grammar from lexicon. In MacWhinney, B. (Ed.) *The emergence of language* (pp. 29–79). Mahwah, NJ: Lawrence Erlbaum Associates, Publishers.

Bates, E. & B. MacWhinney (1989) Functionalism and the competition model. In MacWhinney, B. & E. Bates (Eds.) *The crosslinguistic study of sentence processing* (pp. 3–76). New York: Cambridge University Press.

Becker, A. L. (1983) Toward a post-structural view of language learning: A short essay. In *Language Learning 33,* 217–220.

Elman, J. (Undated manuscript) Connectionism, artificial life, and dynamical systems: New approaches to old questions.

Diller, K. (1995) *Language teaching at the millennium: The perfect methods vs. the garden of variety.* Unpublished manuscript.

Gleick, J. (1987) *Chaos: Making a new science.* New York: Penguin Books.

Larsen-Freeman, D. (1991) Teaching grammar. In Celce-Murcia, M. (Ed.) *Teaching English as a second or foreign language* (pp. 279–296). Second edition. New York: HarperCollins.

Larsen-Freeman, D. (1995) On the teaching and learning of grammar: Challenging the myths. In Eckman, F., D. Highland, P. Lee, J. Mileham & R. Rutkowski Weber (Eds.) *Second language acquisition theory and pedagogy.* Hillsdale, NJ.: Lawrence Erlbaum Associates, Publishers.

Larsen-Freeman, D. (1997) Chaos/complexity science and second language acquisition. In *Applied Linguistics 18(2),* 141–165.

Larsen-Freeman, D. (2000a) Grammar: Rules and reasons working together. In *ESL Magazine, January/February*, 10–12.

Larsen-Freeman, D. (2000b) An attitude of inquiry: TESOL as science. In *The Journal of the Imagination in Language Learning*, Volume 5.

Larsen-Freeman, D. (2002) *Teaching language: From grammar to grammaring.* Boston, MA: Heinle & Heinle Publishers.

MacWhinney, B. (Ed.) (1999) *The emergence of language.* Mahwah, NJ: Lawrence Erlbaum Associates, Publishers.

Mohanan, K.P. (1992) Emergence of complexity in phonological development. In Ferguson, C., L. Menn & C. Stoel-Gammon (Eds.) *1992: Phonological Development* (pp. 635–662). Timonium, MD: York Press, Inc.

Rutherford, W. (1987) *Second language grammar: Learning and teaching.* London: Longman.

Thornbury, S. (2001) *Uncovering grammar.* Oxford: Macmillan Heinemann.

Notes

[1] Portions of this talk have been drawn from Larsen-Freeman (2002).

[2] A fractal is a geometric figure that is self-similar at every level of scale.

[3] In fact, David Nunan and I gave a paper at the 1997 TESOL Convention on 'grammaring and gardening' to underscore the organic quality of grammar. We were able to find a number of analogies between the two processes.

[4] The notion of simple systems elaborating rather than mimicking the input has been discussed by second language acquisition researchers as well, such as Pit Corder, Ferguson, Andersen, and Schumann.

[5] What I meant was that we need something analogous to the mechanical–meaningful–communicative continuum that has been used to classify form-based drills.

[6] Editor's note: Construction grammar views phrasal patterns as well as words as learned pairings of form and meaning, or 'constructions'. Simple syntactic patterns, or 'argument structure patterns' are seen as imbued with meaning – i.e. the constructions themselves carry meaning independently of the words in a sentence. See Goldberg, A. E. *Constructions: A Construction Grammar Approach to Argument Structure.* (U of Chicago 1995)

2.2 Teaching ESP: How text corpora can help

Gunther Kaltenböck and Barbara Mehlmauer-Larcher

University of Vienna, Austria

ESP is an ever-expanding domain because of the status of English as a *lingua franca* in fields such as science, technology, business and economics, and international relations. ESP has become an area of great interest for EFL teachers, opening up new career perspectives.

Despite its importance, ESP is often neglected in teacher education. Instead, it has been left to the individual teacher to develop his/her own expertise. The diversity of the field in terms of content makes it impossible to prepare trainees for all possible 'S's in ESP. However, expertise on the content level is not the main issue, as this is something that will gradually be developed through teaching practice. Instead, the focus should be on strategies of how to approach ESP texts, by drawing on one's language expertise and applying it in language pedagogy. Therefore, the emphasis should be not so much on content knowledge, but on developing knowledge in the areas of *language description*, which comprises the lexical, grammatical and textual levels, as well as ESP-related *methodology*, focusing on principles of course design, needs analysis, and materials (see diagram below). These two areas are linked in that insights gained from language description have an influence on aspects of teaching.

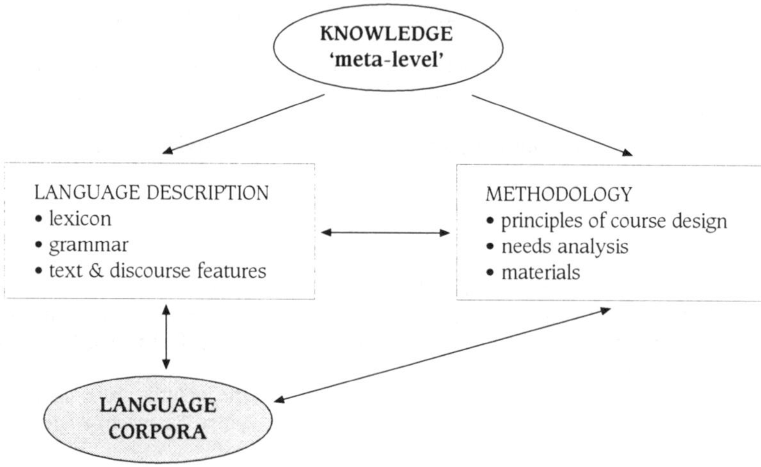

As indicated in the diagram, there is also an important third factor, which is directly linked with that of language description but also has a bearing on methodology, i.e. language corpora. For language teachers computer corpora have various advantages:

- quick and easy access to selected language features in authentic texts
- information not available in dictionaries or grammar books such as fully contextualised examples with information on occurrence in text type and frequency
- a source of empowerment for the teacher (especially the non-native), but generally for all those who are not experts in a given content area

The following examples (derived from the ICE-GB corpus) illustrate the three levels of language description:

- **Lexical level**: for instance, collocations (e.g. of the lexical item *insurance: take out ~, ~ against sth, ~ property banking …*) provide interesting insights, which, however, still need to be processed for teaching and learning purposes.
- **Grammatical level**: for instance, the use of *would* in *if*-clauses in business letters, often ignored in grammar practice books
- **Text level**: for instance, moves (i.e. unit of text that expresses a specific communicative intention) in business letters, e.g. letters of rejection. On the basis of various examples of this text type we can generalise and identify a fairly fixed pattern of moves, e.g. Salutation – Contextualisation – Rejection – Softening – Thank you – Closing. From a pedagogic view, this analysis can easily be converted into teaching material.

To sum up, corpora have great potential for language teaching, specifically for ESP. They provide interesting data for language description of ESP texts, which, however, need to be carefully processed and transformed for application in language pedagogy.

E-mail: gunther.kaltenboeck@univie.ac.at
barbara.mehlmauer-larcher@univie.ac.at

2.3 Making effective use of corpus-derived data: the AWL

Sandra Haywood *University of Nottingham, England*

For students on EAP programmes, rapid vocabulary expansion is one of the keys to success. In their vocabulary learning, many students focus on the salient terms of their specialist field; this is worthwhile, of course, but in so doing they tend to miss the general academic vocabulary, which is equally, if not more, useful. I suggest using The Academic Word List, available at: http://www.vuw.ac.nz/lals/div1/awl, to identify and prioritise the words commonly found in academic contexts, thus providing principled guidance on vocabulary study.

The AWL is a list of 570 headwords created from a corpus of written academic texts, which occur relatively frequently across disciplines. It is a valuable resource for teachers of EAP mixed-discipline classes, since it enables a focus on vocabulary, which is important for all students, no matter which academic field they intend to study.

I have developed two computer programs which facilitate materials development using the AWL. A text pasted into the AWL Highlighter, available at: http://www.nottingham.ac.uk/~cczwood/cgi-bin/acwordlist.html, will be processed to show all words from the AWL highlighted in bold (see example paragraph below). The AWL Gapmaker, available at: http://www.nottingham.ac.uk/~cczwood/cgi-bin/AcademicGap.html, replaces words from the AWL with gaps.

Basing my **approach** on Nation's claim that three **processes** are **required** for effective vocabulary learning: noticing, retrieval and generative production, I have developed the following **procedure**:

1 Use a text for reading comprehension and skills work.
2 Re-present the now familiar text, with all words from the AWL highlighted.
3 Support vocabulary development through worksheets, each focusing on one word or one word family from the AWL.
4 Recycle some of the academic vocabulary studied, using gapped summaries of the original texts.

Step 2 is very simple, yet useful in that it gives students principled guidance over which vocabulary items to spend their time on, and encourages noticing of the target vocabulary within its context. The worksheets in step 3 are built around the study of concordance lines to provide multiple encounters with the target word in a variety of contexts. This encourages students to look long and hard at new words, to become aware of typical patterns of use and to pick up on frequently occurring lexico-grammatical phrases. For guidance I provide questions which direct students to look for certain features. Prompts to encourage productive generative use are also useful. Such worksheets provide a model of how to engage with a new item of vocabulary that students can carry over to their independent study. Step 4 requires retrieval of previously met vocabulary, reinforcing memory and strengthening learning.

This approach to vocabulary teaching focuses on items which represent core vocabulary for all EAP students, thus supporting and facilitating their vocabulary development, in terms of both breadth and depth.

I am currently working on making the Highlighter and Gapmaker available in a format to facilitate students' independent use.

E-mail: sandra.haywood@nottingham.ac.uk

2.4 Weaving some lexical threads

Nick Hamilton *International House, London, England*

The presentation considered the following threads of working with a lexical approach as a way of achieving an integrated methodology:

- Sound Chunking (my term for Phonological Chunking)
- Lexical Chunking
- Grammaticisation
- Reformulation
- Learner Skills

With each of these we looked at materials ranging from Elementary to Advanced level, and discussed the principles behind them and how they could raise awareness of language as lexis, and lead to students becoming more independent.

Sound Chunking

This is the most basic type of chunking and is particularly valuable for low-level students. It is about how we phrase spoken text and how we breathe in a language; it's what gives each language its own distinctive sound. We looked at chunking part of a tapescript as a follow-up to a listening activity, in which students decide where to pause in the text and which words to stress. We also looked at the text of a joke and how it can be chunked and used to build confidence and fluency in speaking.

Lexical Chunking

Here we considered the usefulness of the distinction between chunking for tone units and to encourage students to notice whole chunks of language, the lexical item together with its grammatical pattern. Although there is some overlap, there are also important differences, the main one being that sound chunking tends to separate the lexical item from its grammatical pattern. Chunking a paragraph of a text students have read is a good introduction to this. This is a technique to be used selectively, and it is more suited to Intermediate level and above.

Grammaticisation

This is a way of drawing students' attention to the managing function of grammar over a whole text, and it results in a broad Focus on Form, as opposed to pre-determined discrete items (Focus on FormS). Practically, this can be done with any text which students have processed for meaning, presenting them with a de-grammaticised version of it or part of it. This involves removing word endings, articles, auxiliaries, and most prepositions. Students work collaboratively to grammaticise the text, which is then compared to the original. Surprisingly, perhaps, this seems to work equally well with higher and lower levels.

Reformulation

This is an alternative to traditional 'error correction'. It's interesting to note that many grammatical errors appear as students are forced to paraphrase when they don't know a lexical item. So the focus here is on the 'intended meaning' rather than the 'surface form', giving students language that extends what they already know and not just tidying up the grammar. For the teacher this means listening for the language students don't yet know.

Learner skills

Finally, we considered ways of helping students to process language, in particular the use of a lexical notebook. We looked at a framework for this, where the student chooses a format that suits their learning style. The notebooks can then be used regularly as a basis for reviewing language covered.

E-mail: nick.hamilton@ihlondon.co.uk

2.5 What have corpora ever done for us?

Hugh Dellar *The University of Westminster, England*

The use of computers to analyse language has revolutionised language teaching, and corpus linguists have become an ever-increasing presence at IATEFL and other conferences. Obviously, much good has come from this. We have a new generation of improved dictionaries, containing better information about usage, collocation and frequency; superb new reference books have been made possible, and, perhaps inadvertently, corpus linguistics has helped to launch the Lexical Approach, and thus to move language back into the centre of language teaching. Nevertheless, despite these advances, corpus linguistics has also had several negative side-effects.

Central amongst these is the notion that frequency is of prime importance. Frequency can only tell us what is frequent in the bank of English as a whole, not what is useful in particular contexts or conversations, not what is necessary for any given student, not even what is teachable. Many very infrequent words – *collocation*, *salt*, *traffic jam* – may actually be vital to learners from an early stage. Furthermore, corpora at present deal only with frequent words – not with collocations or multi-word phrases. The process of lemmatisation[1] distorts things further both by suggesting that two-word items such as *dark horse* are actually examples of *dark* and *horse*, and also by treating plural nouns as further examples of singular ones. We need to know not just that *get* is frequent, but also which uses of it are more frequent than others. Frequency can also be skewed by data, as proven by one major corpus's suggestion that one of the most common collocates of *thaw* is actually *John*[2]!!

A further issue is the fact that corpora are based on native-speaker English samples. Such data is of marginal relevance to learners, particularly lower-level ones, for whom input needs to be carefully graded and selected, and for whom the best texts may well be those scripted specifically for them. Corpora are unable to provide scripted prototypical dialogues or texts for us, and to insist on their primacy is to deny the ability of teachers to produce such key classroom materials.

I also believe that current corpora hamper non-native speaker teachers. This happens partly due to the attention corpora linguists pay at talks to neologisms and quirks, which make English more of a foreign language to non-native teachers than is wise. Furthermore, the fact that corpora are native-speaker databases means that the language of fluent non-native speakers is disregarded, despite its obvious value for learners.

A final problem lies with the argument that corpora are not only useful for showing us the error of our ways, but also for checking that our hunches are right. This implies that we are only right once we have checked, and thus de-skills teachers and overlooks the intuitions about language that we bring to our classrooms. The time has come for teachers to reclaim their right to make statements about language based on their own experiences of it, and to no longer feel dictated to by flawed corpora-based commercial products!!

E-mail: lisasjukur@easynet.co.uk

Editor's notes

[1] A lemma is an abstract lexical category consisting of a lexeme base plus its inflected forms, which share the same part of speech. Lemmatisation is the process of identifying the frequency of words in a corpus whereby every inflexion of a word is given a frequency number denoting how many times per corpus size this particular form of the word occurs.

[2] John Thaw – a well-known British TV and stage actor.

2.6 Teaching vocabulary and pronunciation in combination: A challenging approach

Katerina Nicolaidis and Marina Mattheoudakis
Aristotle University of Thessaloniki, Greece

In line with the current philosophy of integrating skills and language components, this study proposes a unified approach to the teaching of vocabulary and pronunciation. In the Greek EFL context, vocabulary is taught independently of other language components, most commonly through well-known techniques, e.g. sense relations and lexical sets.

However, pronunciation is neglected for a number of reasons, including teachers' own limited pronunciation training, lack of confidence because they are non-native speakers of English, time and resource constraints, and prioritisation of other language components. A renewed interest in pronunciation teaching is necessary so as to ensure intelligible, socially acceptable and communicatively functional pronunciation.

As every new vocabulary item gives teachers the opportunity for pronunciation teaching, the proposed approach focuses on how to deal with new words and sounds, how to organise vocabulary so as to reinforce memorisation through common sounds and how to introduce new vocabulary items on the basis of common and contrasting sounds. The rationale for this approach was presented, together with examples from units of popular EFL coursebooks for beginner and intermediate levels. For beginners, the unit focused on Christmas vocabulary, which provided suitable material for the teaching of vowels. A colour-coding system, adapted from Celce-Murcia et al. (*Teaching Pronunciation. A Reference for Teachers of English to Speakers of Other Languages* CUP 1996), was used, and each vowel of the standard southern British variety was associated with a colour: *green* /iː/, *pink* /ɪ/, *red* /e/, *black* /æ/, *rusty* /ʌ/, *scarlet* /ɑː/, *orange* /ɒ/, *bordeaux* /ɔː/, *sooty* /ʊ/, *blue* /uː/, *purple* /ɜː/, *colourful* /ə/. On the basis of this system, new vocabulary items were categorised according to colour, e.g. the word *tree* was associated with the colour *green* due to their common vowel.

Numerous activities can be designed for practice in the perception and production of sounds as well as the contextualised use of vocabulary and formation of collocations. This approach facilitates the teaching and learning of the meaning and form of new words, raises students' awareness of the relationship between sound and meaning, facilitates the learning of phrases on the basis of common and contrasting sounds (e.g. *green bean* vs. *green bin*), assists memorisation of vocabulary and pronunciation through the creation of vivid images (e.g. *blue moon, orange frog*).

At intermediate level, the vocabulary of the unit focused on countries, nationalities and food. The pronunciation focus was the teaching of /s/, /ʃ/, /z/, /ʒ/, /tʃ/, /dʒ/ and stress shift. Nationalities and food were categorized according to common sounds, e.g. *English–Swedish*, *cheese–chocolate*. Various activities were designed for practice, including construction of phrases on the basis of common or contrasting sounds, e.g. *Japanese jam, Russian sauce*.

The steps teachers may follow for the implementation of this approach are:

- specification of vocabulary and pronunciation aims
- categorisation of vocabulary according to pronunciation targets
- enrichment of vocabulary with words that facilitate pronunciation practice
- formation of collocations and phrases: listening–production practice
- use of activities that combine practice in vocabulary and pronunciation

E-mail: knicol@enl.auth.gr
marmat@enl.auth.gr

2.7 Insights into interaction: Doing Conversation Analysis in ESP

Andrew Packett *Instituto de Estudos Jornalísticos, Universidade de Coimbra, Portugal*

Over the last thirty years Conversation Analysis (CA) has developed into a key method for studying social interaction. This talk illustrated how this distinctive research tradition can be seen as a valuable resource for teachers seeking to raise awareness of interactional problems encountered by students in the specialised speech-exchange systems of ESP. Focusing on journalistic interviews, recorded data were presented from both learner and professional contexts used in teaching interview skills to Portuguese students of journalism.

A pedagogic puzzle provided our point of departure: why do learners sometimes sound 'unnatural' when recording face-to-face interviews for radio broadcast? The search for answers involves a detailed consideration of what it means to 'do interviewing' as a collaborative, interactional achievement. As an approach to exploring the data, three 'analytically distinguished but interlocking "organisations" ' (ten Have P. *Doing Conversation Analysis: A Practical Guide.* Sage, 1999: 107) were considered: turn-taking organisation, sequence organisation, and the organisation of turn-construction.

Broadcast interviewing is a pre-allocated turn-taking system with differential distribution of turn-types and roles, and participants' normative orientation to this 'institutional' system can be seen in sequences of talk in which a regular procedure is violated, such as when an interviewee assumes the role of questioner. Such 'deviant case' analysis is useful insofar as the accountable nature of such departures ('so now I'm asking you a question') reveals the participants' awareness of powerful institutional constraints. Learners need to be shown that this is an asymmetrical system in which the interviewer is structurally provided with a relatively powerful role.

The fact that talk is sequentially organised is, of course, a core discovery of CA, and the question–answer sequences of interviews comprise probably the most recognisable form of sequence organisation. Third-position actions (i.e. answer-subsequent turns) assume particular pedagogic importance since this is a prime locus for displaying understanding, and control of, talk. Such actions were shown to be problematic in the learner data, most obviously in the case of disjunctive turns which fail to show awareness of prior talk. More subtly, however, the extracts analysed revealed how learners often fail to align their utterances to the overhearing radio audience as prime recipient of the talk. Use of responsive tokens, such as 'really', 'oh' or 'great', are seen as constitutive of 'doing chat' in that they fail to observe the constraints demanded of the interviewer's 'institutional' role as broadcast journalist. Raising awareness of such interactional problems can be achieved through the noticing of sequential practices common to professional interviews, such as questions which begin by incorporating aspects of prior talk, or which deliberately withhold those responsive tokens typical of ordinary conversation. In this way, comparative use of professional data highlights a basic analytic strategy of CA – '... taking what people are doing and finding out the kind of problem for which this doing might be a solution.' (ten Have 1999:17).

E-mail: apackett@ci.uc.pt

2.8 Tacit misunderstandings: Problems of ellipsis in listening and reading

Ronald Klein *Hiroshima Jogakuin University, Japan*

It is hard to talk about words that are not there. For this reason, ellipsis has been given little attention in grammar texts, let alone addressed as a skill required for competent listening and reading comprehension. These tacit understandings, so second-nature to native speakers, are difficult for EFL students to follow, often leading learners into linguistic wrong turnings and dead ends. Missing words can lead to confusion, when nouns follow nouns, auxiliaries and modals are dropped, verbs are omitted, conjunctions removed and interjections expanded into incomplete phrases. In most cases, the unspoken words have an antecedent referent, which can cause problems for beginner listeners and word-encoding readers.

The first part of the talk was a discussion of the variety of different grammatical and linguistic structures in which words are deleted, including many other forms of substitution and omission, such as block language[1], instructions, headlines, abbreviated sentences, formulae and non-sentences, in addition to Quirk's 'ellipsis' and Celce-Murcia's 'deletions'. This amounts to almost 50 different grammatical forms in all. I call this total corpus of omission 'tacits', since native speakers tacitly understand what is missing and non-native speakers generally do not.

The second point was the discussion of a questionnaire administered to freshman English majors at a Japanese university at the end of their first year. Looking at the 14 sample sentences, only 25.8% of the 53 respondents could restore the deletion correctly in the correct place. Another 20.0% put wrong responses in correct places, 27.8% put wrong responses in wrong places and 26.2% did not answer. That only a quarter of the respondents could correctly fill in the missing words shows that there is a serious problem. This was contrasted with the same test given to higher level professional translators, who scored 82.8%.

Having acknowledged the problem, the third part of the talk was a discussion of how EFL teachers can teach tacits. Several points were made:

1 Tacits are embedded in grammatical structure, and only a firm understanding of base sentence structure will give beginner and intermediate learners the background they need to understand when and where words are omitted.
2 Only by increased and improved exposure to spoken language will students learn to appreciate the flexibility in the language.
3 Some tacits can only be learned by rote, where grammatical coherence is secondary to its operational function. This is certainly the case with aphorisms and the myriad of formulae.
4 Some tacits can be taught with an explanation of where words are deleted in certain contextual situations, elliptical dialogue and non-sentences, similar to omissions of informal speech in the learner's first language.
5 Along with the teaching of base sentence structures, teachers should also teach the parallel possibility of tacits. Other simpler forms of tacits can also be taught by looking for recoverable antecedents when something in the dependent clauses brings linguistic confusion.

These approaches should account for most of the tacits students are likely to encounter. As the data showed, advanced learners do learn what has been deleted and where. This is an expected outcome of greater familiarity with the language and a milestone indicator of being able to use it in its more elastic, informal, common usage.

E-mail: rklein@gaines.hju.ac.jp

Editor's note

1 Block language: 'The form of language used in newspaper headlines, in cables, in notices, on labels of products, and so on. Distinguished by specific rules or patterns, which have developed in part independently of those in ordinary language.' *The Concise Oxford Dictionary of Linguistics* © *Oxford University Press 1997.*

3 CENTRED ON THE LEARNER

3.1 Plenary: Developing learner autonomy – preparing learners for lifelong learning

Leni Dam *Centre for Higher Education, Copenhagen and North Zealand, Denmark.*

This paper deals with the underlying principles, the organization and the contents of a language learning environment where the teacher's professional competence is used to make the learners actively involved in their own learning. It will describe a teaching/ learning situation which has proved effective and useful with learners at all levels. It will take the reader into a language classroom and give examples of activities and tools which have proved useful when preparing learners for lifelong learning. In this connection, the roles and responsibilities of teacher and learners will be discussed. Finally, it will touch upon the problems and successes experienced in this type of classroom setting.

The paper is based partly on my own teaching experiences for more than 25 years with what is now labelled 'developing learner autonomy', and partly on my work in Denmark as well as abroad with language teachers implementing learner autonomy in their own classes.

At the end of the paper there is a short presentation of the workshop that followed the Plenary talk: *How to establish a learner- and learning-centred classroom.*

Introduction: Why is it important to focus on lifelong learning?

For years the literature has told us that real learning only takes place when a learner is actively involved in his or her own learning. Then why is it that this knowledge is not manifest in the FL classroom? We have been told again and again that learners do not necessarily learn what we as teachers believe ourselves to be teaching. Then why is it that the focus still is on teaching rather than learning? Having just returned from Kosovo, where I ran a summer course for a group of Albanian teachers of English, I have once more been confirmed in my theory. I claim that the main reason for the present situation in the FL classroom is due to the many coursebooks that can be seen at any IATEFL conference. They do not support teachers if they want their learners to get involved in and aware of their own learning. They do not help the many teachers who still have to rely on coursebooks due to their own limited competence in English when preparing their learners for lifelong learning – as stressed by John Trim (1988):

> No school, or even university, can provide its pupils with all the knowledge and the skills they will need in their adult lives. Adult life, in its personal as well as its vocational aspects, is far too diverse and too subject to change for any educational curriculum to attempt to provide a detailed preparation. It is more important for a young person to have an understanding of himself/herself, an awareness of the environment and its workings, and to have learned how to think and how to learn.

We know that successful learning takes place when one or more of the following elements are present in the learning process:

- personal involvement/motivation
- a feeling of confidence, security, acceptance, respect
- a feeling of progression
- peer-tutoring
- help and guidance when needed/asked for

This knowledge is based on teachers' own learning experience. During the years 1990–1995 I asked my in-service teachers to think of a personal learning experience they had had at one point in their lives – an activity inspired by Michael Breen when he was working for the Greve Municipality in Denmark (see Breen et al. 1989). The teachers were asked to consider what supported and what hindered their learning. The elements mentioned above are derived from the experience of more than 300 teachers. Apart from supporting the theory about teaching and learning, this activity also makes the teachers realize that they themselves are learners and not just teachers – an important issue if we want them to focus on learning rather than teaching.

In 1976 – as a young teacher of English – I had a group of unmotivated 15-year-olds in my class. I planned and planned and taught and taught. To no avail. It was only when I insisted that the learners took part in the planning that I realized that greater influence/responsibility on the part of the learners in planning and conducting teaching–learning activities led to a greater degree of active involvement/better learning in the actual teaching–learning situation. This again influenced the learners' potential for evaluating the process and at the same time supported their self-esteem. A virtuous circle had been established:

active involvement in the learning process
↓
improved insight into how to learn and what to learn
↓
a prerequisite for self-evaluation
↓
improved self-esteem
↓
increased involvement in the learning process

But not only do we give our learners self-esteem by getting them involved in their own learning. We also provide them with action knowledge, as stated by Douglas Barnes (1976):

> School knowledge is the knowledge which someone else presents to us. We partly grasp it, enough to answer the teacher's questions, to do exercises, or to answer examination questions, but it remains someone else's knowledge, not ours. If we never use this knowledge, we probably forget it. In so far as we use knowledge for our own purposes, however, we begin to incorporate it into our view of the world, and to use parts of it to cope with the exigencies of living. Then it becomes action knowledge.

Again the coursebooks give little help when it comes to action knowledge as opposed to school knowledge. Think of the many coursebooks for beginners still spending paper and time on having learners who have known each other for at least four years asking each other: 'What's your name?' Many teachers claim that their learners like this activity: 'They can say something in English.' My point is that from the very beginning with this activity we make the learners believe that they have to forget what they have learned so far about normal human behaviour. This feeling is supported later on when it comes to learning vocabulary. The teacher will hold up a pencil and ask: 'What is this?' And along the same lines a little later, when it is about time to learn prepositions, the teacher will place the pencil on the table in front of the learner and ask: 'Where is the pencil?' From the very beginning the learner is taught: *You have now entered a FL classroom. Forget that you are normal.* What can be done instead? How can learners be prepared for lifelong learning?

Preparing learners for lifelong learning – the development of learner autonomy

In my view, the development of learner autonomy is one of the solutions – if not *the* solution. I shall try to explain not only why, but also how it is possible to get the learners actively involved in their own learning. But let me first define what I mean by learner autonomy – a definition adapted from Holec (1981):

Learner autonomy is when the learner is *willing* to take charge of his/her own learning, i.e. independently:

- to choose aims and purposes
- to choose materials, methods and tasks
- to exercise choice and purpose in organizing and carrying out the tasks
- to choose criteria for evaluation and using them in evaluation – and when s/he is *capable* of doing so.

Another definition – perhaps less pragmatic – was developed during a workshop in Bergen in 1990:

> ... An autonomous learner is an active participant in the social processes of learning, but also an active interpreter of new information in terms of what s/he already and uniquely knows. It is essential that an autonomous learner is stimulated to evolve an awareness of the aims and processes of learning and is capable of the critical reflection which syllabuses and curricula frequently require but traditional pedagogical measures rarely achieve.

What is important is the fact that we get the learners actively involved in their own learning.

The organisation of the classroom

But how is it done? I will start by describing an autonomous classroom:

> I will define an autonomous classroom as part of a language learning environment in which the learners are given the possibility of being consciously involved in their own learning – and given the opportunity to be autonomous learners.

Notice that I see the classroom as only part of a language learning environment. I am fully aware of the fact that much language learning – if not most language learning – takes place outside the classroom. The learners should at least be made aware of this.

Important issues in this classroom setting are (see Dam, 1995):

- a shift in focus from teaching to learning (see diagram below)
- a change in the learner's role
- a change in the teacher's role
- authenticity
- the role of reflection and documentation
- a view of the language classroom as a rich learning environment.

What we are after is a move from a traditional, teacher-directed teaching environment to a learning-directed learning environment, where teacher and learners enter into an authentic dialogue and in co-operation as regards: what to learn, why to learn and how to learn. A learning environment where the teacher, instead of asking herself how best to teach this or that, asks herself how best to support her learners in learning this or that. A learning environment where the teacher stops asking questions that she knows the answer to. I have tried to describe this situation with the following model:

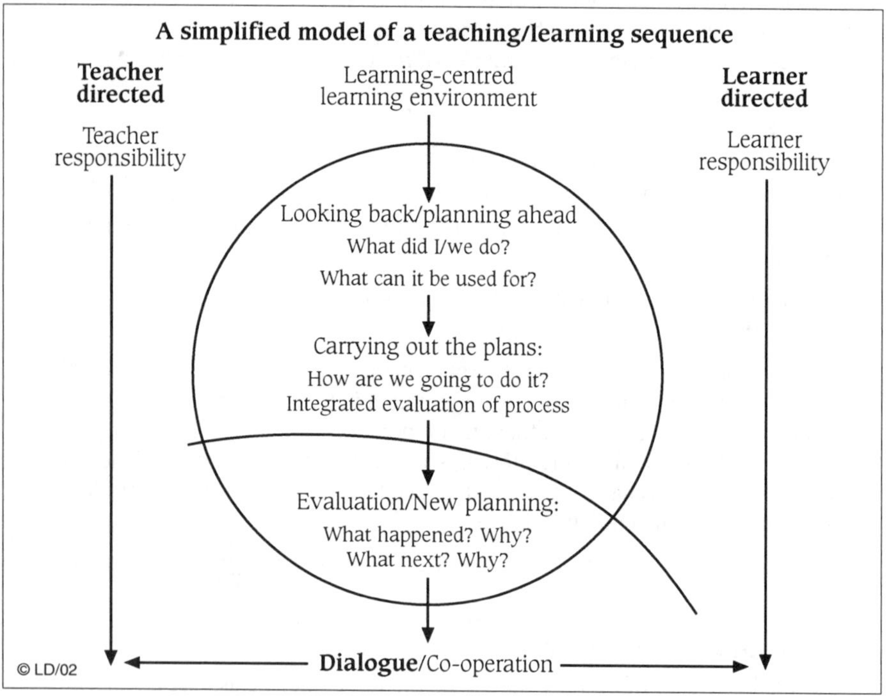

I call this model 'the three circles'. 'The chain' might be a better name for it, but I started out many years ago to use the term 'circles'. I am trying to indicate that it is an ongoing process of unfinished circles interweaving – with evaluation as the pivot.

However, moving from a teacher-directed teaching environment to a learning-directed and learning-centred environment is a long process for teachers as well as learners – a process most difficult for teachers. This move involves what I have called 'Four steps towards responsibility for one's own learning'.

The four steps

experience with and insight into useful and relevant activities, suitable partners, appropriate ways of organising the work undertaken, and various ways of evaluating process as well as progress

↓

awareness of what, why and how to learn – awareness of own role in the learning process

↓

influence on and participation in decision making as regards own learning (choice of activities, partners, materials, etc.)

↓

Responsibility for own learning

In order to support teachers in going through these steps, I have developed a possible plan for a teaching/learning sequence consisting of three clear-cut sections:

1 Teacher-initiated and teacher-directed activities promoting awareness-raising as regards:

- the learning environment and the responsibilities expected from participants
- useful language learning activities

In this section the teacher is in charge. The first type of activities might include questions such as: Why do you learn English? How do you learn English? What is good group work? What is a good teacher? What is a good learner? What do you think you are good at? What would you like to become better at? etc. All of them are activities where the answers will build upon the learners' previous knowledge and will form the basis for the future learning environment. The second type of activities will be activities introduced for the learners to be involved in when later on they are involved in their own language learning.

2 Learner-directed – and learner-initiated – activities:

- Share homework in pairs or groups.
- 'Two minutes' talk.'
- 'Free', learner-chosen activities in groups, in pairs or individually within the given framework and making use of the activities introduced under section 1.
- Plan homework – and perhaps next steps.
- Evaluation of work carried out – individually as well as in pairs or in groups.

In this section the teacher's role is primarily to be a co-learner – a participant in the learning process. What I have entered under section 2 is to a large extent a kind of agenda for the learners to follow when they take over responsibility for directing their own learning. Later on they will set their own agenda.

3 A 'together session' including:

- Presentation and evaluation of results from group work, pair work or individual work.
- Joint events with language input and language activities such as videos, songs, lyrics, storytelling, talk-shows, quizzes, etc. – also including jokes not spoiled by being prepared for language teaching!
- Joint overall evaluation of the session.

The contents of the lessons

One of the most essential things in my view is to get the learners involved in their own personal learning from the very first moment they enter the foreign language classroom. The questions mentioned above – Why do you learn English? What is a good teacher? etc. – are examples of this. At the same time they are examples of authentic communication between teacher and learners. At beginner level – in the very first week – I get the learners involved in real communication among themselves in the following way. I ask them to think of questions that they would like to ask their friends – questions that they do not know the answers to. They write these questions in their logbooks in Danish. I collect the questions and translate them into English. From this list of questions – our own questions – they can now ask and answer in pairs instead of asking: 'What's your name?'

Examples of questions in one class were:

- How do you say *hund* (dog) in English?
- What do you do at home?
- What did you do at home yesterday?
- Have you got an uncle?
- How tall are you?
- How are you?
- Are you OK?
- Do you like (playing football)?
- Which pet do you like best?
- Who are you a fan of?
- What is your favourite food/subject/colour?

If I look at my plan for the first four weeks at beginner level, the following activities support the learners' active involvement in as well as their awareness of their own learning:

- Bring something English to the classroom.
- Write about **yourself**.
- Find at least five words in the picture dictionary that **you** would like to learn/ remember.
- Watch a video – which words did **you** remember?
- **Your** ideas for homework?

This brings me to the importance of the teacher's criteria for choice of activities introduced during the teacher-directed section of a period. On top of what I have mentioned already and of course taking curricular guidelines into account, I will add the following criteria:

- Do they give scope for satisfying the individual learner's needs, interests and potential?
- Do they activate the learners' existing knowledge and at the same time expand this knowledge?
- Are they are open to different learner input and different learner outcomes?
- Do they give scope for a possible feeling of progression?
- Do they give scope for learner–learner interaction, co-operation and peer-tutoring?
- Is it possible to make use of the same 'activity' at different levels, e.g. at elementary level as well as at intermediate level?
- Will the products be useful for other learners and not just for the teacher?

Most coursebooks will activate the learners' existing knowledge, but very few activities will expand this knowledge. Neither will many coursebooks involve the learners in real communication. Some of the data collected from our LAALE (Language Acquisition in an Autonomous Learning Environment) project show this. The following extracts from a collection of peer-to-peer talks from a traditional German class (1) and the autonomous class (2) in the second half of the second year of English show the tendency (Legenhausen 1999):

(1)
S: Ehm, how old is your father?
I: My father is forty years old. And how old is your father?
S: Fifteen years old. How old is your mother?
I: My mother is thirty-nine years old.
S: How old are you?
I: I'm twelve. How old are you?
S: I'm eleven. What are your foreign languages?
I: My foreign languages are Sport, Textil. What are your foreign languages?
S: My foreign languages are Biologie, Textil and German.
I: Ehm.
S: Oh, ah how ah how ne, what is the name of your father?
I: The name of my father is Felix. And what is the name of your father?

(2)
L: What should we talk about, Carsten?
C: I don't know, we could talk about our music group [?]
L: Yeah, that's a good idea –
C: I think it's fun. Now we have to play, ah, record our tape.
L: Yeah, the first time.
C: Yes, it's very exciting. I have made a cover to our tape at home.
L: That one you showed me?
C: Yes.
L: The only thing it's beautiful.
C: Beautiful?
L: Yes.
C: It's lovely. (Laughing)
L: I think it's good, too.
C: Yes.

(1)

J: I'm going to have a family with two ehm chil childrens, and I'm going to live in a big house.

I: When is your birthday?

J: My birthday is now.

I: Ah, my birthday is on the sixteen ah ja of ehm of May. When is your sister's birthday?

J: My sister's birthday is in is on the twenty-seventh of February.

I: What films do you like?

(2)

D: ... What did/what should you do today?

L: Today I ehm I shall have my birthday.

D: Have you birthday today?

L: Yes.

D: Happy birthday.

L: Thank you. So I should home and, and and make made a cake to my –

D: Birthday cake?

L: Cake, yes, so I should have this cake and, so to, afternoon my eh my friend is coming and my Dad and Mum's friend is coming too, so I should have birthday [?]

The classroom setting

A traditional language classroom is to a large extent teacher- and/or teaching-centred. The following characteristics can often be found there:

- Tables and chairs are placed in rows or in a U-shape so the learners face the teacher and vice versa.
- The teacher makes use of a coursebook. Its use is directed by the teacher: one lesson or chapter at a time for the whole class.
- Additional materials are often teacher-designed or at least provided by the teacher.
- In general, materials are supposed to facilitate teaching.
- Communication mainly takes place between teacher and learners.

As opposed to this setting, a learner-centred and learning-centred classroom is characterized by:

- An environment facilitating learning.
- A setting where the learners are facing each other.
- A setting which leaves space for the teacher to be engaged in group work as well as individual counselling.
- Learner–learner interaction and communication.

If we look into the classroom, we can see that the tables are placed in groups seating four to six learners, which means that each learner is seated with three to five peers. This setting has got a number of advantages:

- It makes quick discussions and exchange of views within a group possible.
- It calls upon learner activity and peer tutoring.

- It supports individual learner involvement, as it is less threatening to talk in a small group than in an open forum.
- It makes a transfer of focus from the teacher (traditionally 'the entertainer') to the participants possible and thus facilitates learner–learner interaction.

A video extract from an autonomous classroom

At this point an extract from my video 'It's up to yourself if you want to learn': Autonomous language learning at intermediate level – was shown. The extract showed a class of 14/15-year-olds planning a project about England and the English. It showed the organisation of group work; it showed teacher and learners at work; and it showed a 'together session' with presentations and shared evaluation. It also showed the use of logbooks – learners' as well as teacher's.

Useful tools when developing learner autonomy

The use of a daily logbook has in my view turned out to be the most important tool in the development of learner autonomy for many reasons, some of which I have listed below. The following arguments were collected in 1998 among teachers and learners making use of logbooks in their English classes:

- The use of the diary is an authentic means of learning the language.
- Workbook/notebook.
- Everything in one book.
- A place for demands to be stated.
- Helps the learner to structure his/her work – daily routine, homework, plans for next lesson.
- Documentation for what has been done – learner responsibility.
- A means of communication between learner/teacher/parents.
- A place for registering possible progress.
- A place for self-evaluation.
- The 'structure' on which the logbook is based and used gives space for individual support and guidance.
- Gives the teacher good insight into the individual learner's way of working, linguistic strengths and/or weaknesses, etc.
- A means of awareness-raising for the learner as well as the teacher.
  (Teacher's arguments)

- It helps you to become better at English (writing, spelling, expressing yourself).
- It is good to see what you have done.
- It helps you to remember what to do – contracts, homework, plans.
- Only one book.
  (Students' arguments)

Preparing learners for lifelong learning – successes and problems

Has the learning environment described succeeded in preparing the learners for lifelong learning? If we look at the following answer from a 15-year-old girl when the class was asked what they had learned in their English lessons that they could make use of outside school, the answer must be yes.

> I already make use of the fixed procedures from our diaries when trying to get something done at home. Then I make a list of what to do or remember the following day. That makes things much easier. I have also via English learned to start a conversation with a stranger and ask good questions. And I think that our 'together' session has helped me to become better at listening to other people and to be interested in them. I feel that I have learned to believe in myself and to be independent.

If in addition we consider the communicative abilities developed in these learners, there is no doubt in my mind that the language classroom – or any classroom for that matter – should be organised according to the principles described above.

The learning-centred environment develops in its participants – learners and teachers alike – self-esteem which supports them in the actual learning process as well as when coping with other exigencies of life. It caters for authentic, real-life communication.

On the other hand, there is no doubt that developing learner autonomy is a long and hard process for teachers and learners alike. I started out by saying that there is still a long way to go – for many reasons. However, the successes by far exceed the problems encountered, which the following statements also show.

Problems

- Parents' as well as learners' attitudes to and expectations of the teacher: 'It is the teacher's job to teach'.
- Insecurity on the part of the teacher: 'Will they learn enough?' 'What about the weak learners?'
- Difficult to handle with many students.
- Difficult to let go.
- Difficult for the learners to take hold.
- The learners' capacity to take responsibility.
- Difficult to administer. Chaos. Lack of time. Waste of time.
- Curricular demands and tests.

Successes

- Motivation and engagement on the part of the learners.
- Socially responsible learners.
- The teacher's insight into individual learners' needs and ways of learning.
- The learners' linguistic competence.
- The satisfaction deriving from the fact that the teacher has become a co-learner.
- 'The most positive thing about the way I am working now is that I have become a human being in my classes.' (Spanish teacher, 1989)

Concluding remarks

The road towards learner autonomy is long and hard, but also fruitful on both sides. However, if it fails, it is important to remember that the one to blame first of all is the teacher. I have therefore collected in a forthcoming publication (2002) what I call a checklist for teachers to look at before blaming the learners:

- Does the learner know what is expected of him?
- Have I – the teacher – supported the learners in setting up their individual goals/aims/ objectives?
- Have the learners gained awareness as well as experience as regards:
  - what to do?
  - how to do it?
- Have useful tools been introduced into the learning environment supporting the learners' awareness-raising as regards their own learning (logbooks, portfolio, and posters)?
- Have I – the teacher – entered into a dialogue with my learners – a dialogue that enhances rather than hinders learner autonomy? Have I stopped asking questions that I can answer myself?

In short:

- Have I prepared the learners for taking responsibility for their own learning?
- Have I managed to establish a learning environment that supports self-esteem for learners and teacher alike – an environment which supports personal development for its participants?
- Have I prepared my learners for lifelong learning?

(Dam, *The development of learner autonomy – the teacher's responsibility* [forthcoming])

Workshop: How to establish a learner- and learning-centred classroom

The plenary talk had to a large extent been concerned with the more theoretical aspects of the development of learner autonomy. The workshop was intended to give the participants – novices as well as teachers already engaged in the development of learner autonomy in their classes – a chance to discuss 'how to establish a learner-centred learning environment' – and problems as well as successes in this connection. Video extracts from autonomous classrooms as well as examples of learners' logs were the starting points for discussion among the participants: Which problems have we experienced or do we foresee? Which successes have we experienced or do we foresee? Questions and areas to be discussed/tackled in this connection during the workshop were then collected and formed the content of the workshop.

References

Barnes, D. (1976) *From Communication to Curriculum*. Harmondsworth: Penguin.

Bergen report on *Developing Autonomous Learning in the Foreign Language Classroom*. Bergen: Universitetet i Bergen, Institutt for praktisk pedagogikk (1990).

Breen, M., C. Candlin, L. Dam & G. Gabrielsen (1989) *The evolution of a teacher training programme*. In R. K. Johnson *The Second Language Curriculum* Cambridge: Cambridge University Press.

Dam, L. (1976/1982) Teaching heterogeneous classes – why, how, with what results? (mimeo in Danish). Copenhagen: The Danish Ministry of Education.

Dam, L. (1995) *Learner Autonomy – From Theory to Classroom Practice*. Dublin: Authentik Language Learning Resources Ltd.

Dam, L. & J. Lentz (1998) *It's up to yourself if you want to learn – Autonomous language learning at intermediate level*. Video/Print material, The Royal Danish Institute of Educational Studies (DPU), Copenhagen. [The video can be ordered from: bogsalg@dpb.dpu.dk]

Dam, L. (1999) Dennis the Menace – and Autonomy. In Missler, B. & U. Multhaup (Eds.), *The Construction of Knowledge, Learner Autonomy and Related Issues in Foreign Language Learning. Essays in Honour of Dieter Wolff.* Tübingen: Stauffenburg Verlag.

Dam, L. (1999) How to develop autonomy in a school context – how to get teachers to change their practice. In Edelhoff, C. & R. Weskamp (Eds.), *Autonomes Fremdsprachenlernen.* Ismaning: Hueber Verlag.

Dam, L. (2001) Bridging the gap between real life and the language classroom principles, practices and outcomes. In Wagner, J. (Ed.) *Pædagogik og læring i fremmed- og andetsprog.* Odense working papers in language and communication. No. 22 January 2001.

Dam, L. (Ed.) (2001) Promoting learner autonomy – new insights. In *AILA Review 15.*

Dam, L. (2002) Developing learner autonomy – the teacher's responsibility. In Little, D. (Ed.) *Towards learner autonomy: learner, teacher, educational institution.* Dublin: Authentik.

Holec, H. (1981) *Autonomy in Foreign Language learning.* London: Pergamon.

Legenhausen, L. (1999) Traditional and autonomous learners compared. The impact of classroom culture on communicative attitudes and behaviour. In Edelhoff, C. & R. Weskamp (Eds.), *Autonomes Fremdsprachenlernen.* Ismaning: Hueber Verlag.

Trim, J. (1988) Preface. In Holec, H. (Ed.) *Autonomy and self-directed learning: present fields of application.* Strasbourg: Council of Europe.

3.2 Assessing your learning style

Marjorie Rosenberg *Pädagogische Akademie, Graz, Austria*

Why do certain activities work well in one language class but not in another? This often has to do with the learning styles of the individuals. Using material developed by April Bowie, of Seattle, Washington, participants had the opportunity to explore their learning style preferences. The introductory activity, 'Look Inside Your Brain', was followed by a survey which indicated both primary and secondary style preferences.

The basic premise of this learning style model deals with how we perceive and organise information. Some of us understand the world around us through our five senses and others through our thoughts and feelings. After we have taken in the information, we then go on to organise it in a linear or a random manner. Looking at these four combinations we find four distinct learning styles.

The first style dealt with was the 'Power Planner'. These people take a sensory inventory and then organise the information in a linear fashion. They tend to be logical, practical and well-organised. They prefer learning step by step and need grammar rules and structures. They like routines and become stressed by lack of organisation. Teachers can help them by letting them know what material will be covered, giving them practical examples on how to use the language and specific feedback on their work.

The next style was the 'Expert Investigator'. These people reflect on relationships between concepts and ideas and organise information in a linear fashion. As learners they enjoy research. The group work often done in language classes can be stressful for them, as they need more time for self-reflection. As perfectionists, they may have difficulties with deadlines. Teachers can help them by trying to answer all of their questions or providing them with sources where they can look things up themselves.

We then discussed the 'Flexible Friend', who reflects on relationships between people and ideas, and organises information in a random way. These learners usually enjoy group work and learn best in a comfortable and friendly atmosphere. They need to find personal connections to the material and feel stressed if they are not allowed to work with their friends or have to compete. Teachers can help them by using co-operative language learning activities and giving them the chance to express their feelings in the foreign language.

The last style covered was the 'Radical Reformer'. These learners take a sensory inventory and then organise information in a random manner. They like to be considered unique and are often seen as being adventurous. They prefer real-life experiences for learning and enjoy role-plays and the chance to try out the language they are learning. They become stressed when they feel they have no choices. Teachers can help them by providing lessons with variety and allowing them to be creative.

Participants discovered for themselves that this model could be helpful in creating functioning groups and give them more opportunities to understand and meet the diverse needs of their students.

E-mail: mrosenberg@aon.at

3.3 Group collaboration as a tool to aid learner autonomy

Fiona McKeand *The British Council, Thailand*

Students who choose their own objectives and strategies, monitoring their own progress, gain maximum benefit from a course. As decision-makers and designers of materials, students become empowered and develop a greater awareness of the learning process. Group collaboration, as a learning tool, improves class dynamics, creates a pool of ideas and knowledge, encourages reflection and feedback, and accelerates language acquisition.

Peer and self-awareness questionnaires increase tolerance of differences in learning strategies, and students discover rationale from someone other than the teacher. Experimentation and feedback on the different learner strategies found within the class are encouraged.

Collaborative goal setting is a powerful aid to group cohesion. Each week, pairs of students discuss their learning achievements and problems. This mentor system, introduced early in a course, provides each individual with an ally, drawing reliance away from the teacher. As their acquaintance develops, students set tailor-made and achievable short-term learning goals for their partners, based on motivation, particular concerns and available time. Besides the obvious pedagogical benefits, gentle peer policing means that students help each other to develop time management, decision-making skills and teamwork, all skills relevant to business and life outside of formal education.

In trouble-shooting sessions, specific learning problems are discussed by the students, who then pool resources and tips. Besides greatly reducing the feeling of struggling through the language alone, advice from peers who have experienced and overcome the same problems can be more resonant than from a native speaker teacher who cannot totally empathise.

In discussions around a set topic, learners choose associated vocabulary they wish to practise, sharing words in groups and explaining meaning. The teacher models pronunciation where needed, and helps with queries. Students then write their words on

Post-it notes on their desks as visual prompts during the discussion. This method can also be used for focusing on difficult grammar points or pronunciation areas, encouraging students to activate new language or work on specific problem areas. In this way, students see the course working for them on a practical, personal level.

Through student-as-teacher language presentations, individuals or groups choose, research and present language from the syllabus to their peers, with the teacher on hand as guide during the planning, and to provide follow-up work after the presentation. Students can present an area they are confident in, or use the opportunity to work on a personal weakness, thereby boosting their confidence considerably. Another learner can assume responsibility for summing up the language points covered in a lesson and inviting suggestions for further learning.

Students can provide further input and simultaneously focus on their own interests by creating worksheets for their favourite films, songs or stories, or collaborate as a class to produce stories or class cassettes. These materials can form a class library or alternatively, they may be stored in self-access rooms for other classes to use, thereby instilling a sense of pride and ownership of the learning process.

E-mail: fiona.mckeand@britishcouncil.org.th

3.4 Reflective journals for monitoring pronunciation improvement

Helen Huntley *West Virginia University, USA*

Teachers on academic English courses often find students in their classes who speak with such poor comprehensibility that their ability to communicate successfully and to participate fully in the academic community is compromised. Such problems have typically been addressed by pronunciation practice, which involves listening to and repeating problem consonants, vowels, and suprasegmentals. However, while students often appear to be successful in repetition, they are rarely able to transfer this practice to real-life situations.

In an effort to enhance the transferability of pronunciation practice, students on academic ESL speaking courses are taught how to monitor and assess their own performance by reflecting on and defining their own objectives for pronunciation improvement, by evaluating their own strengths and weaknesses, and by choosing activities which correspond to their individual goals and personal learning styles. During class sessions, students learn and practise pronunciation features such as word and sentence stress, intonation, focus words and thought groups. These skills are then practised in a choice of out-of-class assignments designed to promote interaction in a situation students are likely to encounter in real life or to identify specific features of native-speaker speech. Students must then submit a reflective journal which includes their personal objective, a short description of the activity, and their reflection and self-evaluation of their pronunciation and communicative skills in relation to the objective of the activity. The following journal extract illustrates how a pronunciation feature learned in class can be transferred successfully through careful self-monitoring.

Goal: To improve teen/ty sounds

In class last week, I learned from the teacher how to make pretty sure what I was saying when I pronounced my social security number. In the past, when I said the number to the bank teller, 8 out of 10 times they would ask is it eighteen or eighty. (My last four numbers 1891.) The reason is that I pronounced my last 4 numbers as eighteen ninety-one. The bank teller would not have a problem with ninety-one but would have problem with eighteen. Sometimes I was at a loss why they could not understand. Now I know the reason and the way to correct it. For the past two weeks, I practised it in a bank and it worked!

In a low-tech environment, journals may easily be submitted in a handwritten form. However, the inclusion of the reflective journals on an online course has lent itself to the submission of the journals by e-mail, voice e-mail, and audio web-board. These alternative environments allow students to share their journals with each other and allow the teacher to respond in written or spoken form. This increased use of technology has resulted in the students producing longer and more articulate reflections on their pronunciation progress.

E-mail: hhuntley@mail.wvu.edu

3.5 Improving editing techniques through learner-centred consciousness-raising activities

Veronica Colwell O'Callaghan *Universidad de León, Spain*

While much research in error analysis has been devoted to identifying and classifying learners' errors, there has been relatively little research to investigate how errors might best be treated in formal learning contexts. Correction and feedback have remained largely teacher-centred, even within so-called learner-centred approaches. A plausible reason for this might just be that effective and efficient learner-centred activities that are compatible with such approaches have yet to be designed.

Numerous recent proposals in the literature suggest that learners' errors in the foreign language represent linguistic growth points and that measures that tap these growth points include: learner-centred error analysis, pre- and post-task consciousness-raising activities, pushed output[1] and language awareness training. In the light of such proposals and calls for research into learner-centred error analysis, we have been conducting ongoing action research for over three years with undergraduate Spanish students of English philology. These students are aiming at very high levels of proficiency in terms of both fluency and accuracy in long-turn spoken and written discourse.

Our study set out to examine the efficacy, or otherwise, of improving grammatical accuracy in long-turn foreign language writing by means of learner-centred error analysis, i.e. independent and collaborative learner-centred analysis of the learners' own errors as opposed to contrived ones. To this end, we initially focused on post-task consciousness-raising activities and pushed output. However, the negotiated, learner-centred syllabus soon indicated that our initial focus was too narrow and the need soon arose to integrate other important aspects into the study i.e., pre-task consciousness-raising activities and language awareness training. Therefore, we extended the aims of our classroom-oriented research to include the identification of the pedagogic variables that might facilitate and/or impede effective editing and self-correction techniques. This implied an exploration of students' attitudes, motivation and previous learning experiences, their interests, expectations and beliefs about writing in general, and, indeed, our own.

Our findings to date, which are qualitative rather than quantitative, indicate that where error treatment is concerned, learner-centred error analysis does indeed have an important role to play in the monolingual foreign language class. The findings suggest that the negotiation that occurs through collaborative learner-centred error analysis is highly effective and efficient in the advanced writing class. By means of this negotiated interaction, learners question others and themselves, observe gaps in their knowledge, share problems and achievements, encourage one another, clarify points, come to notice where they are going wrong, and identify and classify their own mistakes. In short, they carry out their own error analysis. Our findings also indicate that learner-centred error analysis is only effective if and when other specific aspects of the writing process are adequately dealt with. These include a negotiated syllabus, learner-centred language awareness, extensive practice at composing, and constructive criticism. In our study these aspects have in fact proven to be important prerequisites to meaningful, learner-centred error analysis.

E-mail: dfmvc@unileon.es

Editor's note

[1] 'Pushed output' occurs when an activity forces learners to produce more accurate and more complex language. (See Swain, M. 1985)

3.6 A learning-centred syllabus in a Japanese university classroom

Gregory Poole *Takachiho University, Suginami, Tokyo, Japan*

Although often deemed reticent and unresponsive language learners, all Japanese students are familiar with collaborative projects and team learning. In this short presentation of 'work in progress', I began by outlining the reasons why the passive lecture-style of most high school and university language classes in Japan is related to Freire's concept of 'banking education' or to an 'empty vessel' model rather than to the more learner-centered models employed in Japanese primary and secondary schools. I argued that with careful thought and planning, there is every reason to believe that a more flexible approach to the language syllabus could be successful in a Japanese college setting.

My presentation, then, was a proposal for implementing more flexible teaching and learning methods at a Japanese university. First, I discussed the specific context, namely how the realities and attributes of ELT in Japanese schools of higher education fit closely with Holliday's description (*Appropriate Methodology and Social Context* CUP 1994) of Tertiary English and Secondary English Programmes (TESEP) worldwide.

I also explained the local setting of the university where I teach, so that the audience would have a better understanding of the issues facing EFL teachers there. My university is a four-year institution of commerce and management studies, with 2800 undergraduates and a two-year EFL curriculum of both required and elective classes. I feel that the key issues that need to be addressed for our EFL programme are:

- extremely limited classroom/contact hours (40 hours/year)
- lack of continuity between individual classes as well as grade levels
- poor student attendance, motivation and self-confidence
- inadequate intradepartmental communication and staff morale

I talked about how these challenges could possibly be addressed using a more open syllabus. The aim of this syllabus would be for students to learn to work collaboratively on EFL writing projects in a technologically enhanced classroom. I argued that through computer-conferencing media such as computer-assisted classroom discussion (CACD) and computer-mediated conferencing (CMC), students would be able to assume a greater attitude of confidence, one that is more achievement-oriented rather than test-driven. The classroom in which I have been piloting such a programme is equipped with the Daedalus Integrated Writing Environment (DIWE). On a local area network this package seems to have helped to establish an interactive classroom environment that especially enhances the process-based approach to writing. I feel that the objectives of such a syllabus would help to alleviate the different local issues at our university.

I explained that the rationale for using such a flexible, learning-centred, computer-enhanced syllabus is that it would fit with the 'teacher culture' in Japanese universities, especially the common notions of 'guided learning' (*shido kyooiku*) and 'project-based seminars' (*zeminaaru*), as well as the technologically-oriented Japanese college 'student culture'.

Finally, the audience participated in a brief discussion that focused on the possible challenges and hurdles to implementing my ideas. A few participants with experience of teaching in Japan pointed out that there would be a major challenge to such a syllabus from teachers who may feel threatened by change.

E-mail: GregPoole86@alumni.brown.edu

3.7 The Koblenz model within Anglo-American Cultural Studios at German universities

Jody Skinner *University of Koblenz, Germany*

The Koblenz model of Anglo-American Area Studies covers in three semesters eight topics dealing with American and British life, plus selected topics in geography and history (further details at www.uni-koblenz.de/anglistik/subjects/as.html) and uses a technique called Learning by Teaching (full description and bibliography at www.ldl.de) that requires a radical shift in the traditional roles of teacher and learner.

Within a module of three courses students cover the given topics in student-taught lessons and answer 140 questions in Anglo-American geography and history in brief individual presentations. Students meet for consultations to discuss planning for their lesson, the overall topic of which they have chosen during registration for the course. During the consultation session, I take notes about their interests, the questions I have, and the tasks that I give them. We also discuss teaching strategies.

The problem of what content to use in Area Studies is thus to a limited degree passed on to the student-teachers, who – based on our discussions and on what they have read – choose the aspects they consider important for their lessons. After each lesson I meet with the student-teachers and discuss the lesson in detail with them, providing them with copies of my written notes. In addition, they are also required to hand in evaluations of the lesson, with notes about content, didactics and language, which are then made available to their fellow student-teachers.

By giving students the chance to use their English actively in class, I have noticed an increase in fluency, a use of vocabulary that flows naturally, increased self-confidence and after three courses, fundamental knowledge of various aspects of American and British life. Do they actually learn more about area studies by using the Koblenz model? To be honest, I don't know. Empirical data is needed here to make the necessary comparison with traditionally taught courses. Intuitively I assume that learning is easier if it involves as many senses as possible, that active learning is more effective than passive consumption, and that the mere fact of connecting content with different voices and different faces, using different teaching techniques, should make learning more effective.

I have had to adjust my role as teacher, to learn when to keep quiet and how to listen more carefully. The satisfaction I gain from becoming a partner in learning and not just a dispenser of information is invaluable and has made the classroom experience a pleasure for both me and my students. If I were to teach the class in a traditional way, each lesson would be simply my umpteenth performance; for the student-teachers, who are uniformly well-prepared and extremely enthusiastic, it's their opening night. And it's their enthusiasm, their questions, their dedication that keep Area Studies in Koblenz for me as fresh and exciting now as it was when I began the module years ago.

E-mail: jody@uni-koblenz.de

3.8 Students guiding students through the Web

Natalie Cigankova *The University of Latvia, Riga, Latvia*

Many teachers would doubt that the Internet deserves to be considered a reliable source for academic writing at university. The writer argued that students need the teacher's guidance in exploring World Wide Web resources for academic purposes, because a spontaneous, chaotic process of harnessing the Web by students is taking place independently from teachers, causing frequent cases of plagiarism and various citing errors in academic assignments. This paper reports on a project aimed at incorporating information technology (beyond word processing) into the process of developing advanced academic writing skills.

The purposes of the project were to offer students a useful and motivating writing task, to help them develop a critical attitude towards information on the Web, and to encourage them to develop knowledge through collaboration. Starting the project in 1999 with Latvian undergraduate students preparing for writing their first academic papers in English, we aimed at proving that the use of the World Wide Web in academic writing instruction can benefit students and specifically at introducing an activity which can help develop students' Internet academic research skills.

To achieve these aims, students were involved in collaborative project work, exploring resources for student writers on the Internet and writing an *Internet Guide for Writing Students.* Originating from the familiar mode of academic review writing, the activity fosters the process of students' learning to find and evaluate electronic information, compare it with the information from traditional printed library resources and synthesise it in writing website reviews. Similar activities have been described in ELT literature (Dudeney 2000; Sperling 1999, Teeler and Gray 2000); however, we aimed at developing a simple activity of review writing into a full-scale collaborative project connecting generations of students into a community of online learners.

During three academic years, as part of their study programme, the students analysed and evaluated websites that may be of interest for writing students. The procedure consisted of the following stages:

1 Preparation (off-line)
- Developing criteria for website evaluation, such as: consistency, clarity, interactivity, ease of use, loading speed, special features, links to other Web pages and sites
- Preparing handouts or on-line instructions
- Preparing websites for evaluation
- Preparing students – teaching electronic literacy (mouse) skills

2 Web sites analysis and evaluation (students online)
- Finding websites for reviewing
- Reading and evaluating
- Taking notes

3 Review writing (off-line)
- Comparing information on the sites with printed sources and incorporating the analysis into the reviews
- Writing reviews (drafts)
- E-mailing reviews to peers
- Collaborative work: peer editing, discussing and selecting materials for the *Guide*
- Publishing (self-publishing, Web posting)

Students' comments were collected and published to guide the next generation of students through the Web, so that they, in their turn, could contribute to the project and update the information in the *Guide.*

The highly positive results of the project allow the author to recommend this form of instruction as one that is useful, comparatively easy to organise and highly stimulating.

E-mail: ncigankova@hotmail.com

3.9 Student experience in TEFL reform in China

Christina Ng *Hong Kong Institute of Education, Hong Kong, China*

Background

The English teaching syllabus in China was last revised in 1993. Teachers were encouraged to adopt communicative approaches. A new set of textbooks was published for use in all secondary schools.

This research compared two cohorts of university freshman, one of whom (N=748) had learned English in secondary school with the old syllabus and the other (N=645) with the revised syllabus. It aimed to compare their perceptions on learning English at secondary school and at university. The data was collected with a questionnaire administered at two stages, and involved two cohorts of university freshmen (1998–99 and 1999–2000).

Findings

Students were asked to reflect on their views and rank the importance of various language skills based on their reflections on secondary school experience and their current experience at university.

At secondary school, both groups found reading and vocabulary the most important skills. There was no significant difference between the two groups. The importance of reading can be attributed to the text-based tradition of English teaching and learning in China. It was believed that the language could be learnt through in-depth analysis of literary texts. This text-driven teaching and learning approach could be seen clearly in the old textbooks. But the new syllabus had not changed this text-driven preconception.

Moreover, the importance of the public examination produced a strong washback effect on teaching and learning. The public examination had not been revised together with the teaching syllabus. Reading and vocabulary were major aspects of assessment. There was a prescribed vocabulary list in the syllabus. Even with the communicative claims of the revised syllabus, the vocabulary list was still a vital part of the syllabus and the teaching materials. In the public exam, there was another 5% of unknown vocabulary to be assessed. Therefore students felt that they should learn more in order to ensure that they could tackle that 5%.

At university, both groups also had similar perceptions of English language learning. Speaking and listening became the most important skills. Both groups had more exposure to the foreign language (e.g. reading English materials, talking to exchange students). They became more aware of their communicative needs in using the language. However, reading and vocabulary were still in the top ranks among both groups.

Both groups noted a wider range of classroom activities at university. These included discussion, mini-presentations and role-play. Both groups enjoyed English lessons at university more than at secondary school.

Conclusions

1 The fact that the perceptions of both groups were very similar suggests that the impact of the ELT reform on students is limited. Traditional beliefs about language teaching and learning, as well as the washback effect of the public examination, still prevail among students in both groups. The lack of significant differences between the two groups indicates that reform cannot be driven by a new syllabus and a new set of textbooks alone.

2 Learner autonomy is important in the learning process. At university, the students all enjoyed the less controlled classroom activities.

3 At university both groups had developed their awareness of their communicative needs for using the language and this indicates that exposure and communicative activities are vital in the learning process.

E-mail: cswng@ied.edu.hk

4 FOCUSING ON THE TEACHER

4.1 Plenary: Bridging gaps: A dialectic perspective on teacher development[1]

Martha C. Pennington, PhD *University of Luton*

Abstract

Teaching is a process that always involves a balancing of opposing goals and needs. There is no perfect solution to this balancing act, and teachers must be able to constantly shift the balance point between opposing goals in response to changing circumstances and student characteristics. The distance between opposing goals and needs in education creates dissonances and gaps in which learning and change can occur.

Teacher development can be viewed as a dialectic process in which individual teachers bridge gaps in different ways that reflect new knowledge and engagement with voices and worlds outside their own classrooms. In the best case, this dialectic results in novel responses and multiple solutions to the educational balancing act. In the worst case, teachers resist the teaching dialectic by retreating to one or another extreme position or by 'flip-flopping' unsystematically from one extreme to the other.

Introduction

Teaching is about gaps, gaps that need facing, and gaps that need bridging. The gaps exist in the distance between a number of competing factors related to teaching, each of them creating dissonances or schisms of various sorts (Fig. 1).

- The **opposing requirements** of teaching (e.g. process vs. product, structure vs. creativity, individualisation vs. standardisation)
- The **polarising tendencies** of the political process within which education exists
- The **incongruity** between a teacher's goals and those of an administrator or governing body
- The **distance** between teacher and student
- The **contrast** between one teacher's world and another's
- The **conflict** inherent in teachers' isolation coupled with their need for support and connectedness
- The **inconsistency** inherent in the natural tendency to routine and teachers' characteristic desire to 'make it new'
- The **lack of translation and transfer** between old and familiar teaching approaches and new and unfamiliar ones
- The **separation** between 'ideality' and reality
- The **difference** between expectation and implementation

Fig. 1 'Dissonances' or 'Schisms' in Teaching

The tensions inherent in education have been noted by others. In a cross-cultural comparison of teaching concerns in the University of Bristol ENCOMPASS project, teachers in England, Denmark and France described contrasting priorities in their work (Fig. 2). Nias (1993) has observed:

> The feelings associated with teaching seem always to be contradictory. Successful teachers learn to keep them in balance, but even they swing, sometimes by the minute, between love and rage, elation and despair. To 'be' a teacher is to be relaxed and in control, yet tired and under stress: to feel whole while being pulled apart; to be in love with one's work, but daily to talk of leaving it. It is to learn to live with unresolved uncertainties, contradictions and dilemmas; to accept that the very nature of teaching is paradoxical. (pp. 191–192)

• Concern for the 'learner'	*vs.*	Concern for the 'whole child'
• Subject knowledge	*vs.*	Personal development
• High academic achievement	*vs.*	Achievement for citizenship
• Discrete subjects	*vs.*	Cross-curricular projects
• Individual achievement	*vs.*	Group co-operation
• Common achievement level	*vs.*	Differentiated teaching
• Professional autonomy	*vs.*	Collaborative working

(Adapted from McNess, Broadfoot and Osborn 2001, p. 11)

Fig. 2. Affective Contrasts in Teaching

We have to learn to live with paradoxes, contrasting priorities, and gaps. But the trick in teaching is to keep any of these gaps from becoming a yawning chasm! We had better mind these gaps!

A dialectic view of change in education

Baxter and Montgomery (1996) offer a 'relational dialectics' perspective on relationships that involves 'a *ceaseless interplay* between contrary and opposing tendencies' (p. 3) [italics in original]. They describe contrast and oppositions as a vital force in relationships and in society at large, through which individuals and groups define their own unique place and voice in relation to those of others. The reality of communication is thus less one of active opposition of one voice warring against another than one of 'countervailing voices' in 'interactive opposition' to one another (Baxter & Montgomery, 1996, p. 46). Through such interactive construction and development, ever new positions and discourses emerge out of the creative tension of different voices and different points of view, creating new points of reference.

This relational dialectics idea has something to tell us about teacher development. The relational dialectic is one of continually changing and emergent properties growing out of the creative tension inherent in different positions, different voices, different trends. This kind of creative tension offers many possibilities for teachers to grow and change, reflecting attempts to cope with the dissonances, schisms, and opposing priorities represented in Figs. 1 and 2. In the creative tension of contrasting priorities teachers can find new resources for development and change, as they try to balance a range of different forces and factors in their teaching contexts.

Change is always about gaps. It is in the gap that opportunities for change exist. Evolutionary change is a process of bridging gaps, of creating new colours and patterns out of old. Revolutionary change is a more difficult and risky process of jumping across gaps, as when a process-oriented approach to teaching is suddenly replaced by a product-oriented one, or vice versa. Educational systems in respect of the highest level, top-down initiatives are prone to such revolutions, in which the old way is denigrated and re-labelled in negative terms as 'The Wrong Way' and then opposed to some new way labelled 'The Right Way'. More often than not, these are just new labels for old ideas; and like the wolf in sheep's clothing, they will eventually be found out for what they really are.

But in the meantime, they create oppositions which paint the world in black and white terms, and 'invite' (quote–unquote) all teachers to come over to the new 'white' side and leave the old 'black' side behind. What educational authorities are essentially asking teachers to do in such cases is to jump the gap, to leave their old familiar territory behind, and change sides. But this is very risky indeed, and most teachers learn to live with the dialectic tension between their own world of the classroom and directives or initiatives coming from outside.

Maintaining the classroom level teaching–learning ecology in balance while also allowing for situational responsiveness and innovation is the major achievement of classroom teachers, which the entire educational establishment needs to support. Otherwise, teachers may seek to reduce uncertainty and complexity in their work by attempting to avoid the dialectic tensions inherent in the educational process. The tendency to simplify the teaching universe by following one definite method or path no matter what, in our terms, refusing to bridge the gap, is an understandable one, given the incredible complexity of the teaching task. But teacher development requires facing up to the gaps and attempting to develop a teaching framework that can manage them.

Teaching frameworks

I have looked in some detail at how teachers' approaches or teaching frameworks develop and change, or fail to change, over time. I define a *teaching framework* as made up of the four components shown in Figs. 3–5, with each component providing a type of structuring of instruction. The Philosophical Basis provides a structuring of knowledge, beliefs and values about teaching and learning into a set of educational principles. The Curriculum is a plan or guidelines structuring the content, sequence and/or mode of instruction. Materials are developed or selected to structure the presentation of information according to the design of instruction in the Curriculum. The Procedures are actions intended to structure behaviour in a way that will optimise learning.

Philosophical Basis	Concepts structuring knowledge, beliefs and values about teaching and learning into educational principles
Curriculum	Plan or guidelines structuring the content, sequence and/or mode of instruction into a workable design for implementing educational principles
Materials	Texts and other objects (implements, machines, etc.) structuring presentation of information
Procedures	Actions structuring behavior to optimize learning

Fig. 3 Components of a Teaching Framework

Philosophical Basis
→ *implemented in* **Curriculum**
→ *implemented in* **Materials**
→ *implemented in* **Procedures**

Fig. 4 Hierarchical Structure of Components of Teaching Framework

Philosophical Basis	**Concept Structures**	*Cognitive*
Curriculum	**Planning Structures**	↕
Materials	**Presentational Structures**	
Procedures	**Action Structures**	*Behavioral*

Fig. 5 Levels of Structure in a Teaching Framework

In school systems and individual schools, the attempt is often made to develop an explicit *Educational Framework* that establishes consistent relations among these levels, such that the components of a teaching framework form a hierarchical system (Fig. 4). The notion of a Teaching Framework can be also be applied to the description of recognised teaching methods and approaches. Fig. 6 contrasts Structural Language Teaching (SLT) and Communicative Language Teaching (CLT) in terms of the components of a Teaching Framework as developed here.

A *Personal Teaching Framework* is an individual teacher's instructional schema or system for teaching, describable in terms of the components of Philosophical Basis, Curriculum, Materials and Procedures. It includes a personalised or subjective theory of the nature of language learning and language teaching, as well as cognitive structures for problem-solving, and proceduralised routines for behavior and interpretation of classroom events. An individual's Personal Teaching Framework incorporates universal, or near-universal features, as well as personal and culturally specific features. An individual teacher's framework may be a relatively integrated approach or may be a relatively loose collection of components gathered from diverse sources and representing a variety of approaches that attempt to deal with the conflicting priorities and gaps of teaching.

The conception of a Personal Teaching Framework is a more dynamic and less restrictive view of method than that put forward by the classical theorists. An individual's teaching framework is developed, and continually revised, as an interaction of methods knowledge with many other types of information available to the teacher. What was in the classical treatment a static description of the structure of a method becomes instead a description of the nature and the development of the cognitive structures organising teachers' experiences and directing their thoughts and actions.

A Personal Teaching Framework can be described as a multi-level schema (Fig. 5). At the highest (or deepest) level, that of the Philosophical Basis, a Personal Teaching Framework can be characterised as an individual's structure of abstract constructs which organise theoretical and subject matter knowledge. The Philosophical Basis of the framework could thus be described as a set of *concept structures*. At the lowest (or

Structural Language Teaching		Communicative Language Teaching
	Philosophical Basis	
Linguistic knowledge (Language as subject area)	*Educational Goal*	Communicative competence (Language as behavior)
Grammatical system	*Language*	Communicative system
Learn individually	*Learning*	Learn interactively
Transmission of information	*Teaching*	Facilitation of learning
	Curriculum	
Mastery of formal rules, lexis (for examination)	*Learning Goal*	Communicative effectiveness (for life purposes)
Maximize coverage	*Teaching Goal*	Maximize practice
Comprehensive	*Coverage*	Needs-based
Grammatical structure	*Organizing Principle*	Communicative purpose
Constructed	*Content*	Authentic
	Materials	
Simplified	*Complexity*	Complex
De-contextualized	*Context*	Contextualized
Made-up	*Source*	Corpus-based
Teacher-determined and teacher-organized	*Basis*	Learner-determined and learner-organized
	Procedures	
Teacher-led	*Interaction*	Student-led
High	*Structure*	Low
Restricted	*Speaking*	High
Formal	*Activities*	Real/realistic
External	*Motivation*	Internal

Fig. 6 Contrast of Two Teaching Frameworks

shallowest) level, that of Procedures, the framework is organised in terms of behavioral modes regulating the concrete actions performed by the teacher in interacting with students and in managing the constraints of the teaching context. To contrast these with concept structures, they could be termed *action structures*. At the level of Curriculum, the framework is made up of subject matter modules and organising constructs for implementing instruction. These can be labelled *planning structures*. At the level of Materials, the framework consists of modes for presenting the information of the curriculum. These can be straightforwardly labelled *presentation structures*. From this point of view, the intermediate levels of Curriculum and Materials provide conceptual and behavioral links within a Personal Teaching Framework between ('pure') knowledge and (physical) activity.

Change in a personal teaching framework

Teacher change occurs when the teacher's dominant framework, which has been not only *learned* through formal education but also *acquired* (in Krashen's sense) through the life experience of a particular individual in a particular culture, is affected by another framework or frameworks. This other framework, which is apprehended by the teacher as new information, 'shadows' the dominant framework for a time as a non-dominant, 'muted' framework – possibly as a distant curiosity or vaguely understood ideal for instruction (Fig. 7). It represents in a sense the broad outlines of the teacher's current *ideality* or awareness of new ideas and so a direction for the future. It becomes part of the individual teacher's *actuality* only when experienced through attempts to apply it, or some part of it, either in the sense of trying out a new idea (Curriculum, Materials, or Procedures, or some aspect of these) in the classroom or in the sense of trying to explain actual classroom events in terms of the new framework and thus trying to link new practices to higher levels of structure, including the educational principles of the Philosophical Basis. Eventually, the muted framework, one or more of its structures, or a new framework derived from the muted framework that combines features of the formerly dominant framework, may be 'promoted' to dominant status, becoming the schema guiding the teacher's thoughts about and performance of teaching acts, perhaps through a mechanism of increasing activation and reinforcement of its elements, adding increased weighting to its elements and principles.

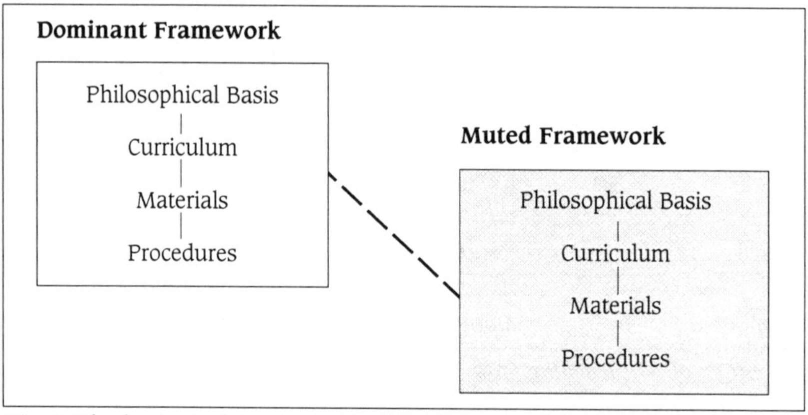

Fig. 7 'Shadowing' of Dominant Teaching Framework by Muted One

Teachers' responses to innovation

All kinds of responses, from one extreme to another as represented in each point of Figs. 1 and 2, and including blends and hybrids of various sorts, are possible in the 'merger zone', or 'tension zone', between alternatives and sides of gaps. In the real contexts of education, these will be continually changing, and may include very dramatic shifts – flip-flops, bifurcations and mutations of all sorts. The end product cannot be predicted in advance, but emerges from the characteristics of the individuals and circumstances involved, often in unexpected ways.

Teachers' attempts to deal with gaps can be seen in their responses to innovations (Fig.8). The types of reactions are schematised in terms of a continuum from a teacher's full-scale adoption of a new teaching framework or approach at one end to a teacher's habitual maintenance of an old framework or approach at the other end. In between these two extremes are various forms of incorporation and non-incorporation of new ideas from a different framework into one's Personal Teaching Framework.

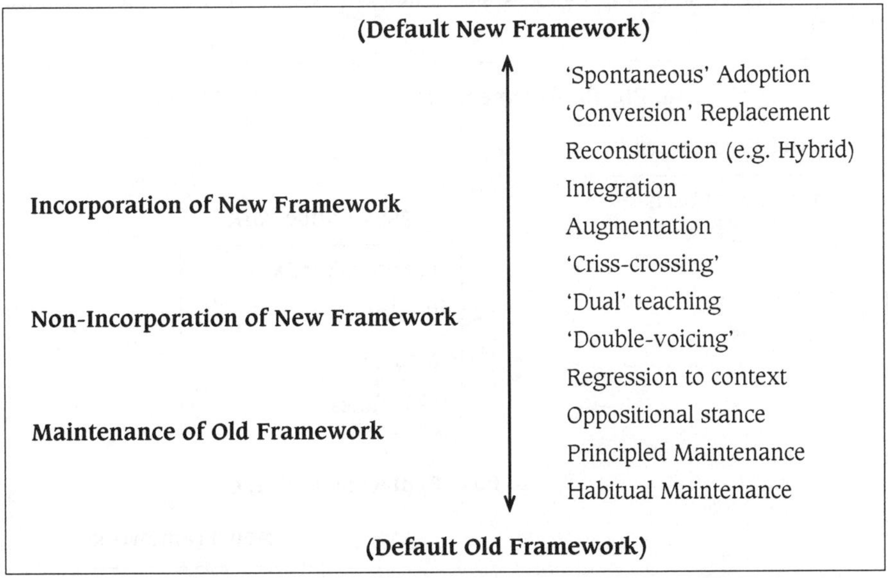

Fig. 8 Teacher Responses to Innovation

'Spontaneous' adoption

At one end of the continuum is what I term a 'Default New Framework' of apparently 'spontaneous' adoption. By this I mean the adoption of a teaching framework by a novice teacher with no experience, based on very strong external influence. For example, in the early 1980s, when I was working in southern California, pre-service teachers in training were being inculcated into Steve Krashen and Tracy Terrell's Natural Approach and in many teacher education courses would not graduate until they could prove that they knew how to implement this approach. In many schools the pressure was also to teach in this way.

'Conversion' replacement

Although not a very common occurrence, it sometimes happens that a teacher abandons a teaching approach entirely, substituting a new framework for the existing one. This kind of *'Conversion'* to a new teaching framework and *Replacement* of an in-place teaching framework by another teaching framework is generally less radical than it appears. The new framework, or a substantial part of it, will usually have become attached to the dominant framework and will have 'shadowed' it in a muted guise, often for many years. Over time, as it becomes more familiar, reinforced by added input about the framework from new sources, the new framework becomes more and more salient. At a certain point of familiarity, it may begin to take more of the teacher's conscious attention, becoming sufficiently dominant for what seems to be a radical replacement of one framework by another. This apparent replacement may in reality be an *upgrading* in the teacher's mind of the status of the muted framework from subordinate to dominant, and a *downgrading* of the formerly dominant framework to subordinate or muted status (Fig. 9).

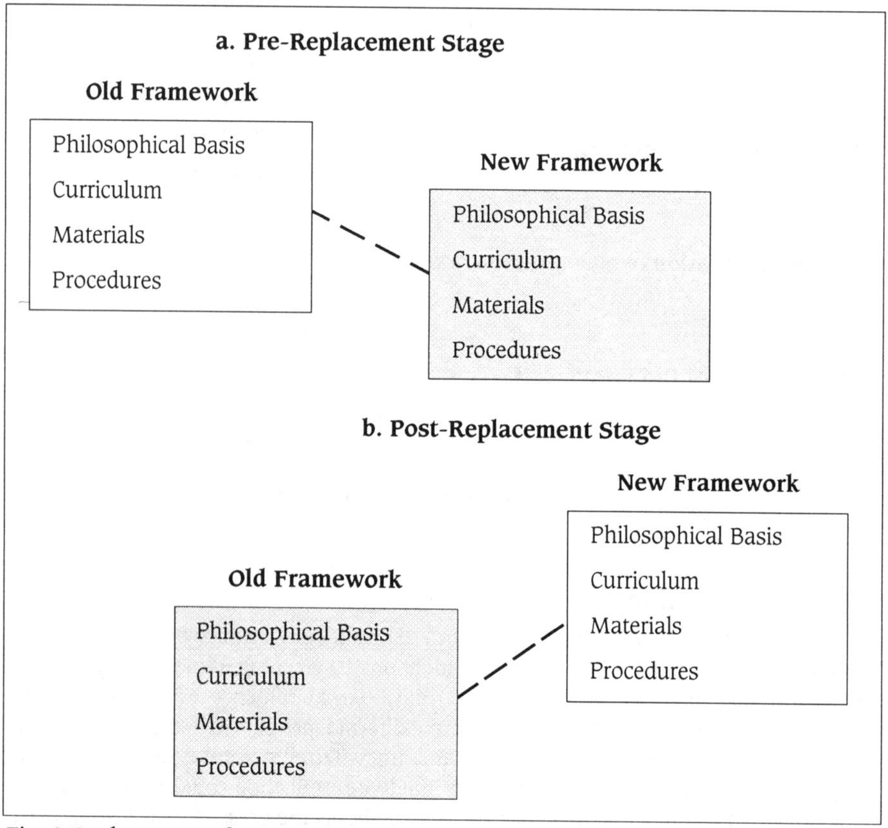

Fig. 9 Replacement of Dominant Teaching Framework by Muted One

Reconstruction

In some cases, teachers may reconceptualise their teaching in light of a newly apprehended teaching approach. This is the most extensive form of incorporation of ideas from a different framework, representing a *Reconstruction* of the framework in terms of new values and practices. A new framework may evolve as an adaptation to input at one of the levels of structure (Philosophical Basis, Curriculum, Materials, Procedures) of the old framework. If this adaptation proceeds to affect the other structures of the framework, it can become a more extensive, higher-level innovation, representing a hybrid method that incorporates hybrid structures at all levels. An example of such a hybrid method is the 'English-with-Cantonese' bilingual teaching method employed by many Hong Kong secondary English teachers. This teaching method involves presenting curriculum content first in English with immediate follow-up in Cantonese (the students' mother tongue) to define new words and explain new concepts. Cantonese is also used for school communication other than lesson content, such as disciplining or making important announcements.

While the origin of this bilingual teaching behaviour may be compensatory (that is, as a response to constraints at the level of Materials and Procedures), it has evolved (Pennington 1995, 1996) for many teachers in Hong Kong as strategic (that is, designed) teaching behavior as part of a Curriculum and has also become invested with a theoretical justification as part of the teachers' Philosophical Basis (Fig. 10a). It can therefore be seen as a *bilingual teaching method* that has evolved as a reconstruction of a dominant English-only educational framework in light of a secondary framework of mother tongue instruction (Fig. 10b).

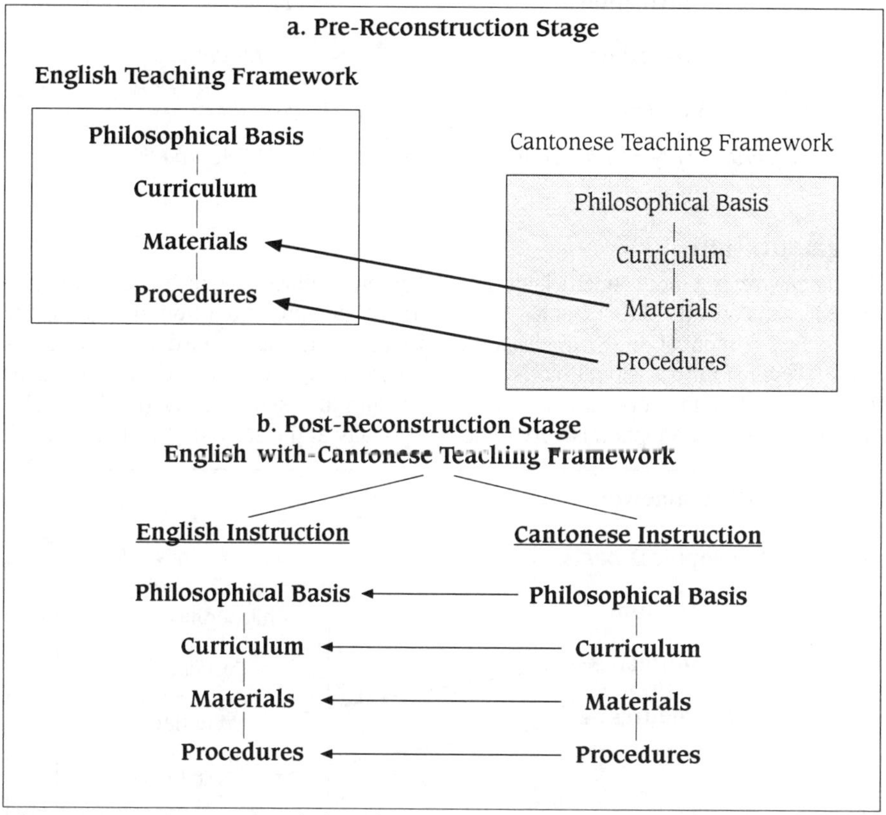

Fig. 10 Reconstruction of English-Only Teaching Framework as English-with-Cantonese Teaching Framework

Integration

A less radical adaptation of a new approach is an *Integration* of some aspect of it into a pre-existing approach. In this sense, the teacher makes an accommodation of an existing teaching framework to a new framework (Fig. 11). An example is the use of CLT components to fulfil SLT purposes, or vice versa. Thus, a teacher whose dominant framework is SLT may use communicative Procedures, such as information-gap or other pair tasks, to fulfil SLT Curriculum goals such as preparing for examinations. Or the SLT-oriented teacher may adapt SLT Materials, such as textbook-based sentence completion exercises, to a CLT philosophical and curricular goal of maximising time for oral practice, by putting students in pairs to talk over the answers to the textbook exercises. To the extent that CLT elements are integrated into the original SLT framework, to that extent is the framework changed by the new elements.

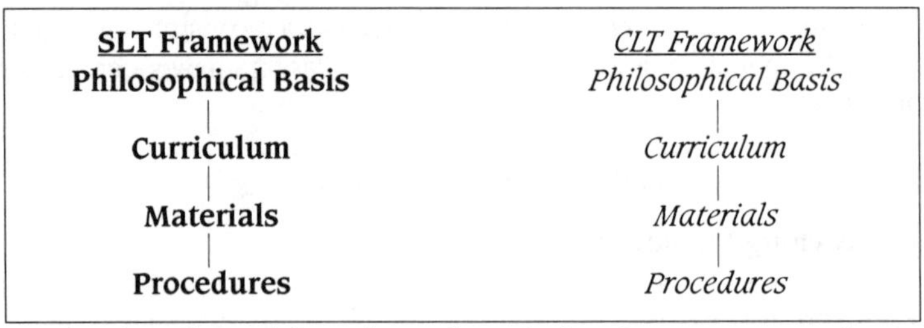

Fig. 11 Integration of CLT Philosophy and Curriculum into SLT Approach

Augmentation

Augmentation is a more superficial form of adoption in which new techniques or ready-made lessons are added to a teacher's 'bag of tricks' and pulled out from time to time to add variety or motivation. Examples are the use of CLT activities added to SLT Materials and Procedures for occasional motivation, or of computer games or free reading added within an SLT framework as a reward for finishing an exercise early (Fig. 12). This 'additive' degree of adoption is very typical, especially at the early stages of adoption or

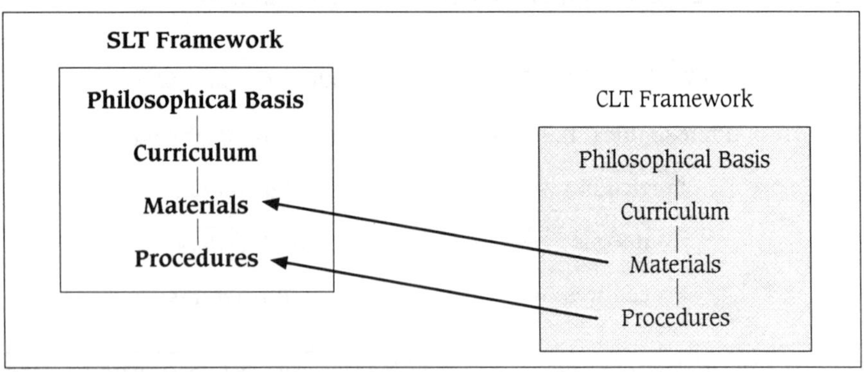

Fig. 12 Augmentation of SLT Framework by CLT Materials and Procedures

awareness of a new approach. At this stage, the new framework can be thought of as 'muted' in comparison to the old teaching framework. Augmentation can therefore be the first step to a more extensive and deeper adoption of an innovation. This is especially likely if the teacher repeatedly makes use of new Materials and/or Procedures, or otherwise recycles and reprocesses information about the new framework multiple times, such as in thinking about its effects on the students or the ways it differs from the old framework.

'Criss-Crossing'

A *'Criss-Crossing'* of approach occurs when frameworks are cross-referenced (Fig. 13). Criss-Crossing at any level makes for an incoherent teaching framework. For example, a teacher who believes in collaborative learning but who must teach according to the National Curriculum may end up with a criss-crossed framework in the sense that the Philosophical Basis is incoherent with the other levels of that teacher's Personal Teaching Framework (Fig. 14).

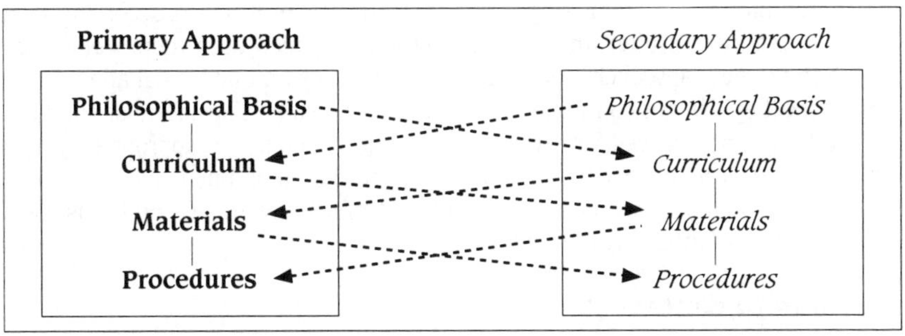

Fig. 13. 'Criss-Crossing' Approaches

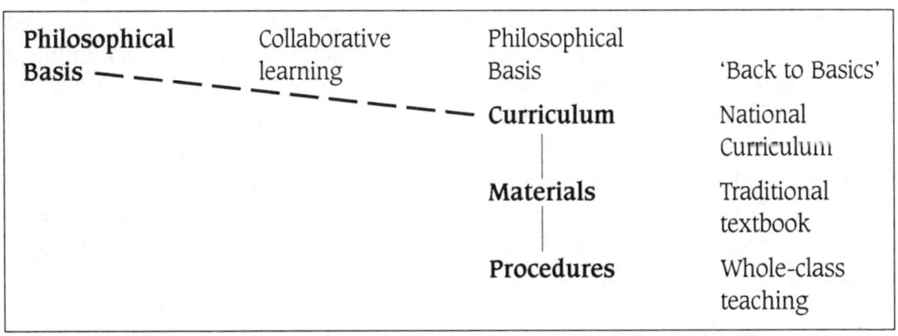

Fig. 14. 'Criss-Crossed' Approach

'Dual' Teaching

'Dual' Teaching is the situation where a teacher feels that two different approaches have value but can find no way to integrate them, and so ends up teaching one sometimes (perhaps for some lessons or some groups of students) and the other one at other times (for other lessons or groups of students). Tsui (1996) describes such a case, in which a

Hong Kong English teacher was attracted to the process approach to the teaching of writing, but was at the same time sceptical about its benefits for her students because of their low English proficiency and problems with English grammar. This teacher ended up teaching some lessons according to the process approach and some lessons in her more traditional grammar-centred approach. I have seen this kind of dual teaching happening today in Britain with the very major shift from learner-centred instruction to whole-class teaching, leaving many teachers struggling to find ways to link the two and in the meantime teaching aspects of each philosophy more or less in parallel, without much linkage between the frameworks.

'Double-voicing'

'Double-voicing' [2] is a response to a new approach in which the teacher espouses a new philosophy and approach on an abstract level but does not teach according to it. An example is many teachers of English in Asia who espouse a teaching ideal of process writing but do not necessarily teach according to this ideal. In such cases, teachers often blame contextual factors as making it impossible for them to teach according to their ideal; but in reality it is often their underlying values which keep them from teaching according to the new approach. Although they may have an intellectual appreciation of an approach, they are not committed to it at a deep level, perhaps because they do not understand it or know it well, or because they do not feel that it is appropriately applied in their teaching situation. Such an intellectual appreciation of a new approach – even a basic curiosity about an approach – represents a degree of awareness and thus could be the starting point of innovation in values and practice.

Regression to context

Sometimes a teacher tries a new approach but rapidly or gradually reverts to the status quo or context of teaching that he or she is used to. An example of such *Regression to Context* is the five beginning Hong Kong secondary school English teachers followed by Pennington and Richards (1997), all of whom quickly abandoned Communicative Language Teaching principles and practices in favour of SLT principles and practices when faced with the reality of examination pressures and a set curriculum, coupled with large classes and audiences of students who spoke a common first language (Cantonese) and who resisted communication in the second language. These teachers can be said to have regressed to context in the sense that they reverted to the Hong Kong transmissional/ prescriptive norm which they would have acquired in their pre-university education in the Hong Kong public school system.

Oppositional Stance

It is not uncommon for teachers to dig in their heels and take a stance in opposition to a new approach, especially one which is being promoted by authorities but which is seen by teachers as significantly different from the existing framework. Such an *Oppositional Stance* often takes on a character of 'us' against 'them' or defines an 'insider' vs. an 'outsider' status within a department, school or teaching group. Because it can be risky job-wise, such 'oppositioning' is usually a late response to curricular changes, after they have been tried for a while by a 'critical mass' of teachers and, as often happens, found wanting. An Oppositional Stance can also be an easy alternative to a full trial of an innovation, perhaps following a premature Regression to Context in the face of the inevitable difficulties and unexpected problems that arise in trying anything new, that is, in trying to bridge the gap between familiar and unfamiliar approaches. I think an example of this is the Oppositional Stance taken by many teachers around the world, who are now forming pockets of resistance to Communicative Language Teaching, though they may in fact have only a low awareness and experience of this approach.

Principled maintenance

Principled maintenance of a teaching framework occurs as the result of a teacher's long experience and high awareness of other approaches but at the same time principled reasons for maintaining the status quo, which may have been developed over a long time. This is a values-based stance of one who has a highly consistent framework with strong links at all levels of structure. An example is maintenance of a process writing framework by a teacher of writing in Japan in the face of great pressure to a product norm. The teacher spends much time and energy trying to convert students to her way of thinking because she strongly believes that this is the correct approach, based on her own experience with process writing on her MA course and in her first teaching job in Hawaii.

Habitual maintenance (Default Old Framework)

The final option is that of habitual maintenance of one's tried-and-true teaching framework, but without any principled reasons for doing so. Such a habitual maintenance of one way of teaching under all circumstances can be described as a form of stagnation or fossilisation.

Conclusion

The extremes of Fig. 8 can be seen as the entry point and exit point of a teaching career. In between are all sorts of responses to the gaps in our work. Teacher development means staying aware of the gaps, which are permanent and can never be closed once and for all. We actually *need* these gaps, and we need to learn to live in the dialectic tension that knows no perfect solution, no right or wrong.

Martha C. Pennington is Powdrill Professor of English Language Acquisition and Head of the Language Research Centre at the University of Luton, and an Honorary Research Fellow at Birkbeck College of the University of London. She has conducted many studies of second language learning and teaching, including projects on the teaching of English in Hong Kong university and secondary school settings, three years' consultancy with the Luton School District, and a Department for Education and Employment project on adapting the Literacy Hour for EAL (English as an Additional Language) pupils. Forthcoming publications include *Language Learning: An Introduction* (Arnold), *Real Language Grammar* (Routledge) and *Introduction to Bilingualism* (Blackwell).

References

Baxter, L. A. & B. M. Montgomery (1996) *Dialogues & Dialectics*. New York: Guilford Press.

Holquist, M. (Ed.) (1981) *The Dialogic Imagination: Four Essays by M. M. Bakhtin*. Austin, TX: University of Texas Press.

McNess, E., P. Broadfoot & M. Osborn (2001) Is the effective compromising the affective? Paper presented at the British Educational Research Conference. University of Leeds. September 2001.

Nias, J. (1993) 'Changing Times, Changing Identities: Grieving for a Lost Self'. In *Educational Research and Evaluation: for Policy and Practice.* (Ed.) R. G. Burgess, 139–156. London: The Falmer Press.

Pennington, M. C. (1995) 'The teacher change cycle'. In *TESOL Quarterly, 29*(4), 705–31.

Pennington, M. C. (1996) *Modeling Teacher Change: Relating Input to Output*. Research Monograph 5. English Department, City University of Hong Kong. (revised version under consideration by publisher)

Pennington, M. C. (1999) *Developing a Personal Teaching Framework*. Luton School District Consultancy.

Pennington, M. C. (2001) Teachers' Responses to Innovations in English Language Teaching: Insights from Research in Hong Kong. Plenary Speaker. Tenth Anniversary Conference on BA and MA TESL Programs. English Department, City University of Hong Kong. June 2001. Revised version of talks given at Thames Valley University, 1997, and University of Reading, 1998.

Pennington, M. C., & J. C. Richards (1997) 'Re-orienting the teaching universe: The experience of five first-year English teachers in Hong Kong'. In *Language Teaching Research, 1*(2), 149–78.

Said, E. (1978) *Orientalism.* New York: Random House.

Tajfel, H. (1981) *Human groups and social categories*. Cambridge: Cambridge University Press.

Tsui, A. B. M. (1996) 'Learning how to teach ESL writing'. In J. C. Richards & D. Freeman (Eds.), *Learning to Teach Second Languages*, 97–120. Cambridge: Cambridge University Press.

Notes

[1] This paper is an abbreviated version of the plenary of the same title given at the conference. The material is from a book based on Pennington (1999, 2001) that is under consideration for publication, entitled *Evolving a Personal Teaching Framework: A Guide for Teacher Reflection and Change*.

[2] The notion of 'double-voicing' comes from the work of Mikhail Bakhtin (Holquist 1981).

4.2 What makes language teachers different?

Simon Borg *University of Leeds, England*

Much recent research into the practices and thinking of language teachers has definitely expanded our understanding of what language teaching involves. However, whilst this work has identified much that is *characteristic* of language teachers, little has emerged which is *distinctive*. An examination of these distinctive features thus seems to be a logical extension to existing research, and the focus of this session was on discussing what the defining characteristics of language teachers might be.

The starting point for the discussion was the following list of characteristics:

- Cognitively mature learners engage in conceptually undemanding activities.
- ELT methodology is more progressive than other subjects.
- Incorrect learner output in language teaching is more acceptable.
- Language teachers are compared to native speakers.
- Language teaching is a political activity.
- Oral production plays a central role.
- The subject and the medium for teaching it are one and the same.
- The subject matter of language teaching is harder to define.

I asked participants to discuss the extent to which they felt these characteristics were distinctive of language teachers. The ensuing discussion suggested that parallels for many of these could be found in other subjects. In craft subjects, for example, such as woodwork, cognitively mature learners engage in basic woodwork tasks which are not conceptually demanding; oral production, too, was not felt to be particularly unique to our field, as getting students to speak is an important part of many other subjects. The discussion also indicated that several of the statements in the above list reflected an exaggerated view of the importance or complexity of language teaching vis-à-vis other subjects; for example, there seems to be no legitimate basis for arguing that the subject matter of language is harder to define than that of, say, history or science; and claiming that language teaching was more 'progressive' was also seen to be problematic.

In the second part of the discussion, participants considered additional ways in which language teachers might be distinguished. Many additional characteristics emerged from this discussion, some of which I list below:

- Whereas in most other subjects, incorrect 'output' or 'products' by the learner are not acceptable, in language teaching 'errors' are seen as a natural and even desirable part of the learning process.
- Language teaching is the only field where teachers may be teaching a subject that they never formally learned at school. This applies to native-speaker teachers.
- Professionally trained non-native language teachers are often compared unfavourably to native speakers, even when the latter are not professionally trained. Similar situations do not occur in other subjects.
- In language teaching, the subject and the medium for teaching it are one and the same, especially in multi-lingual groups where English is the only common language. In no other subject are the content and the medium for teaching it one and the same.

The next stage in examining this issue will be to draw up a revised list of defining characteristics for language teachers and to ask subject specialists outside language teaching whether they feel these characteristics apply to their subjects, too. This outside perspective will complement the views from the inside I have obtained so far from language teaching professionals.

E-mail: s.borg@education.leeds.ac.uk

4.3 The shape of the language teacher

Costas Gabrielatos *Lancaster University, England*

Introduction

There are two broad views on what makes a language teacher effective. One focuses on teachers' language and methodological knowledge/skills, the other on teachers' personality. Here I present a framework which:

- reconciles these views, giving equal weight to all elements
- proposes a way to visualise their interrelations
- takes into account research findings indicating that teachers' practices are mostly influenced by their *interpretation* of methodologies.

Elements

I have expanded Julian Edge's term 'person-who-teaches' into 'person-who-teaches-language'. Each word points towards an indispensable element in a language teacher's profile (Fig. 1).

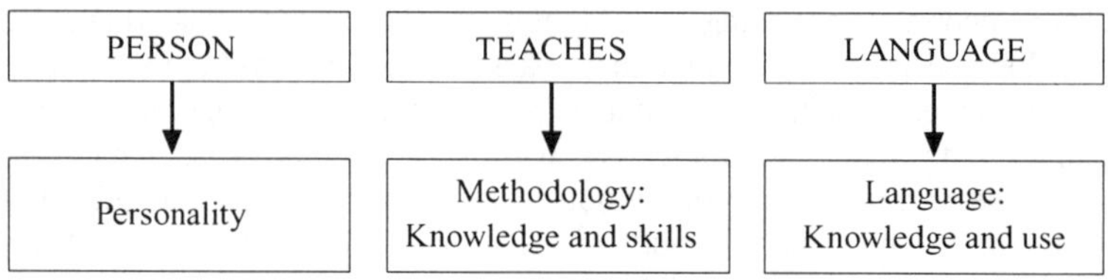

Fig 1

The following tables show the key aspects of each element.

Personality

• Self-awareness • Interpersonal skills • Ability to observe, think critically, use experience • Sensitivity to context	• Attitude towards change, development, diversity, quality, co-operation, authority • Perception of learning, teacher/learner roles, development

Methodology

Knowledge	*Skills*
• Views on methodology • Available materials • Own views on learning/teaching	• Seeing implications of theory • Planning and teaching • Balancing support and challenge • Action research

Language

Knowledge	*Skills*
• Views on language • Awareness of own views on language	• Own language use • Ability to see the implications of language analysis, draw conclusions from own contact with language • Sensitivity to learners' language level

There is some overlap between the elements. For example, teachers' perception/knowledge of language will influence their teaching; their general level of self-awareness will affect their awareness of their beliefs about language/learning.

Interrelations

This framework depicts a teacher's effectiveness as the area of a triangle, with each side representing the degree of development of an element (Fig. 2). The larger the area, the higher the effectiveness.

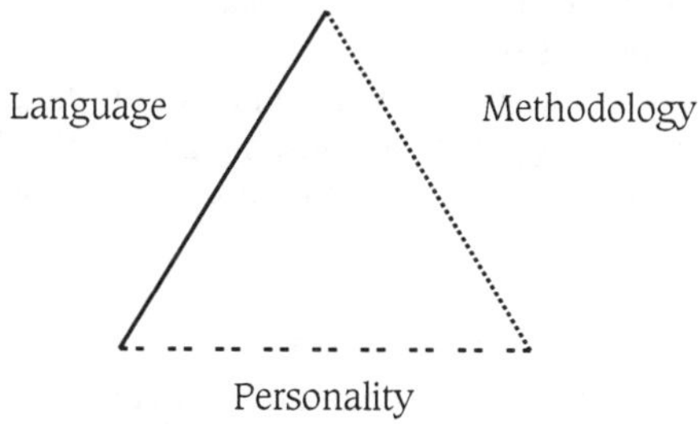

Fig. 2

Apart from comparing different triangles, it is also helpful to compare the sides of individual triangles, that is, examine the *relative degree of development* of each element.

1 **All elements are *equally* developed**. They are utilised to their full capacity and combined to maximum effect (Fig. 2).

2 **One element is far *less* developed**. The less developed element limits the effect of the others (Fig. 3). This representation can also explain why teachers using different methodologies show comparable success: combinations of different levels of development can produce equal triangles.

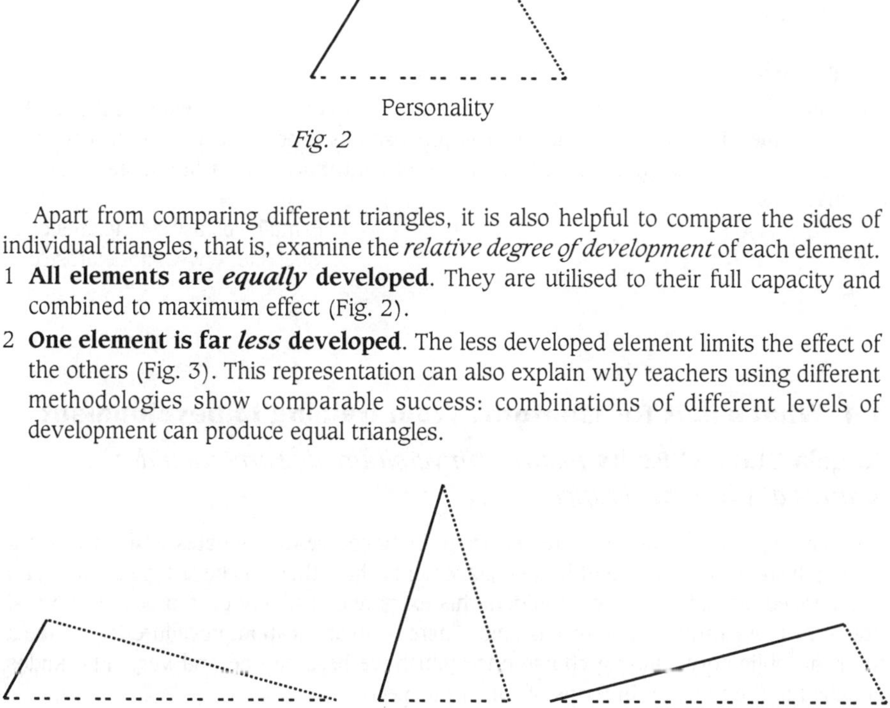

Fig. 3

3 One element is far *more* developed. The more developed element cannot be fully utilised (Fig. 4).

Fig. 4

Some observations

An equilateral triangle will have the largest area of any triangle of the same perimeter. This can be seen as a metaphor for the benefits of well-balanced development.

It is essential that all three elements are above a 'threshold of acceptability'. True, such cut-off points are arbitrary, but such thresholds are already used in education and in determining entrance to professions.

Limited/faulty language knowledge will communicate inaccuracies. Inappropriate methodology will make learning too time-consuming and may discourage learners. An uninterested or offensive teacher will offer little support and few opportunities, and may demotivate learners.

Reservations

The triangle framework is a crude representation of the complex interrelations that make up the profile of a language teacher. It is proposed as a point of departure, a way to visualise the interaction of the basic elements contributing to a language teacher's effectiveness.

E-mail: costas@gabrielatos.com
Website: www.gabrielatos.com

4.4 What's in it for mentors? From training to development

Angela Blazy-O'Reilly *Institut Universitaire de Formation des Maîtres d'Auvergne, France*

Our institute offers a one-year pre-service training course to graduates wishing to work in French state education. Within their placement school they will be assigned a tutor, an experienced practitioner who shoulders this extra responsibility on top of their normal hours. A small annual allowance is paid. There is no application procedure to become a tutor, no obligatory training course once you have become one and very little kudos attached to the function in terms of career prospects.

The Department of English has set up a programme (nine hours of workshops over a year) aimed at showing how an involvement in training can be an ideal mode of professional development. In a state system currently trying to implement a constructivist approach to learning while remaining largely indebted to the knowledge-transmission model, an attempt to analyse accepted mentorship practices and to experiment with new ones has proved beneficial to both tutors and tutees.

We identified two key areas: class observation and feedback sessions.

1 Observation practices

After a number of awareness-raising activities (What do you *think* you are doing? What are you *actually* doing? What *could* you be doing?), tutors practised making transcripts of lessons which were primarily of use to the tutee. The advised format is an exercise book which remains in the possession of the tutee and becomes a record of progress. Separating the *objective* from the *subjective* (dividing the page in half) has been found to be extremely useful for leading the post-observation feedback session.

2 Feedback attitudes

Feedback nearly always takes place immediately after the observed lesson. Many teachers are unaware of the risks involved, in particular in terms of the roles the two partners will unconsciously be led to play. This is the moment of greatest variance with the tutor's teaching persona: they must resist the temptation to prescribe, decide and assess, and think more in terms of supporting, guiding and fostering reflection. The tutee, too, will apply pressure on the tutor to 'be the teacher' and give them the answers.

Inviting the tutee to read silently through the notes taken during the observation (but hiding the *subjective* elements) and waiting for them to react first has been found to be an excellent way of promoting reflexive attitudes. Conclusions are drawn jointly and recorded in the exercise book, together with resolutions taken by the tutee for future lessons.

Conclusion

Tutors acknowledge that adopting such procedures and attitudes has helped them become better listeners and work more efficiently in a team. They learn the benefits of nurturing or fostering learning as opposed to instructing and feel what it is to loosen the reins on a learner, to move from guidance to freedom. All these things are, of course, of great help to them as teachers themselves.

E-mail: ablazy@auvergne.iufm.fr

4.5 Concept maps to trace conceptual change in pre-service English language teachers

Thomas Farrell *Nanyang Technological University, Singapore*

It is now widely acknowledged in general education that pre-service teachers come to teacher education courses with prior beliefs and values. These beliefs have been accumulated from a variety of sources and may act as filters to what they are exposed to in the teacher education programme. Bearing this in mind, it is crucial for teacher educators to establish a reliable means of evaluating the success of their courses. How can teacher educators evaluate what students have learned as a result of taking a course?

Traditional methods have included examinations (both oral and written) and end-of-course questionnaires. Another method available to language teacher educators who are interested in tracing conceptual changes in pre-service teachers as a result of taking a course, is the use of concept maps.

The study outlined in this paper attempted to trace conceptual changes to pre-service teachers as a result of taking an English Reading Methods Module. The students were all pre-service students enrolled on a one-year programme, the Postgraduate Diploma in Education (PGDE), to certify them as secondary school teachers in Singapore. Students follow a ten-month programme in which they experience teaching practice and theory classes. The Reading Module consists of nine classes (18 hours) of instruction on reading theory, teaching strategies and current concepts.

Concept mapping is a research technique for capturing and graphically representing concepts and their hierarchical interrelationships. Pre-module concepts were elicited as a diagnostic tool in order to gauge the students' prior beliefs and knowledge of the reading process, and the teaching of reading. Joram and Gabriele (1998: 176) argue that it is essential that 'teacher educators take prior beliefs into account because any new material taught will have to compete with, replace or otherwise modify the folk theories that already guide both teachers and pupils.' Post-module concept maps were also elicited at the end of the course as an evaluative tool to document students' understanding of the main features of the reading process and what it means to teach reading to secondary school pupils in Singapore. The trainees were then asked to consider any changes between their pre-module concept maps and post-module concept maps. Trainees were asked to write short descriptions of changes and the reasons for these changes on their post-module concept map.

Results show that the course had some impact on the trainees. Many of the students in the module internalized the information presented to them in different ways as represented in different types of concept maps. Detailed results indicate that information gathered from concept maps might be useful to inform teacher educators about how the trainees internalise the curriculum. This knowledge also contributes to a clearer evaluation of the course. Furthermore, concept mapping (pre- and post-module) is useful because it encourages both teacher and students to reflect before and after the course.

E-mail: tscfarre@nie.edu.sg
farrec@hotmail.com

4.6 Mental modelling in a teacher education course

Susmita Pani *English Language Teaching Institute, Orissa, India*

My presentation described a study where the technique of mental modelling (Duffy, Roehler & Herrmann 1988), which is used for development of reading strategies, was tried out in a teacher education context. In recent years, with the focus on learners in the classroom, strategy training has received a great deal of attention. Reading being a very important skill in the Indian context, learners need to develop the strategies to make them more successful readers.

Mental modelling is a teaching technique that informs the learners about the reasoning processes that underlie strategic reading. The teacher uses this technique to show the 'novice' learner, the 'how' of reading by thinking aloud as s/he negotiates for meaning through the text. Thus the reader is able to get a glimpse into the mind of a 'superior' reader. Recent emphasis on the strategic aspects of reading and the role of metacognition in reading make it vital that the reading process should be made explicit for the learner. While teachers are expected to be proficient readers in the language they teach, in India, the non-native teacher's limited skills make it difficult for him/her to develop these skills in their learners. The present study therefore tried out this technique on a teacher education course in India to develop the reading strategies of the trainees. Thirty-five in-service teachers teaching at secondary level were involved in the study. After an initial session to familiarise them with the technique, the actual study began. In groups, trainees tried to guess the meanings of the unknown words in four short texts. They then listened to the mental modelling of their tutor while she did the same tasks. After this, while continuing to work in their groups, trainees tried to identify the strategies used by the tutor. This was followed by a whole-class discussion of the content of the tutor's mental modelling and the merits of this technique. Data was collected through transcripts of the mental modelling of the tutor, trainees' discussion in groups and the retrospective notes of the tutor.

On the basis of the transcripts, evidence of the following strategies was discernible:

- reading the text as a whole before focusing on the parts
- purposeful attempts to puzzle out the meanings of the difficult words
- conscious use of background knowledge
- attempts to establish a relationship between parts of the text.

In addition, these sessions strengthened the trainees' belief that a reader could be helped with reading problems through this technique. In all the four sessions where I used this technique, trainees showed a great deal of interest in doing these tasks. In fact, when I was modelling the reading process, they became so involved that they started to assist me in understanding the process by offering clues. They were also able to suggest how they could use this technique in their own classrooms, thus showing signs of positive development.

E-mail: susmitapani@yahoo.com

4.7 Support and challenge: Effective teacher training from an interpersonal perspective

Rachael Roberts *Solihull College, England*

This workshop came out of my experience of training on CELTA and DELTA courses, and of training trainers. I outlined some situations I had encountered, which seemed very familiar to the participants: trainees who respond to feedback with tears, anger, resentment, inappropriate use of humour, silence and excuses. Such defensive responses are natural in a threatening environment, but are we as tutors sufficiently prepared to deal with them? Equally, could we do more to avoid provoking such responses in the first place?

UCLES' most recent criteria for trainers-in-training include:

- giving feedback 'appropriately and sensitively (according to different personality types)'
- listening skills

- appropriate intervention during feedback
- managing peer feedback
- tact
- counselling skills

While I value the recognition of these skills, it seems to me that a good deal more needs to be said within the profession about what these skills are exactly, and how we can develop them.

We began by exploring listening and counselling skills. Some listening skills that trainers need, I suggested, were:

- making eye contact and showing by posture/body language that you are listening
- asking questions and rephrasing to check that you've really understood
- listening to both the content and what may lie beneath – e.g. a trainee may be expressing anger towards you, but what lies beneath is fear that they aren't good enough

Other counselling skills could include:

- managing boundaries – how close you get/how time is managed, etc.
- owning your opinions and being non-judgmental, e.g., not 'It was a mistake to ...' but 'Doing X meant that Y happened'
- challenging and confronting without being aggressive or punishing
- putting yourself in the other person's shoes
- being aware of one's own limits/competence

In addition, I would like to add a third area – personal development. This could include:

- accepting that you can't always (ever?!) be 'SuperTrainer'
- being 'available' – not preoccupied with your own fears/stresses. This can be facilitated by:
  - taking care of your own needs
  - knowing how you can be wound up by others ('sore spots')
  - asking for help when you need it

Next, I went on to consider how these skills can be developed in the trainer-in-training. I suggested three possible ways: through a reflective journal, through observation tasks on feedback given and through structured supervision, and gave examples such as this journal task:

> Think about a group member you like.
>
> - Why do you like them? Do they remind you of someone/yourself?
> - How does your liking them affect the way you respond to them?
> - How are you when giving them feedback?
> - How much time have you spent with them in comparison with other members of the group?
>
> Now do the same for a group member you either don't like or don't feel particularly interested in.

I also considered ways in which threat, and therefore conflict, could be reduced, by looking at how the process could be made more transparent to participants through discussion and tasks on feedback, exploring concerns openly.

The response from this workshop confirmed my belief that this is an area ripe for further exploration, and I would welcome any feedback or comments.

E-mail: rachael.roberts@solihull.ac.uk

4.8 Meeting trainees' needs – a more reactive approach to CELTA timetabling

Nick Baguley and Julie Constantine *The British Council, Bahrain*

The starting point for our presentation was a newspaper article which described how London's National Theatre had a special studio where actors, directors and writers could rehearse and experiment without being watched. The article included the following quotes:

- 'I need to test it out before I know if it's any good.'
- 'To take the pressure off is very releasing.'
- '... you've got nothing to lose.'

It seemed to us that these statements could just as easily have come from CELTA trainees talking about unobserved teaching practice. As a result we started to look more closely at the idea of rehearsal and experimentation. A study of recent end-of-course evaluations revealed these thoughts from trainees:

- 'A couple of sessions on preparing practice activities and then trying them out on peers would have helped me a lot.'
- 'I would have found it useful to have a follow-up input session with peers to practise things like eliciting, concept checking and drilling before doing it for real.'
- 'It was hard being observed all the time.'
- 'I would have enjoyed some more unobserved TP.'
- 'I felt that input sessions should be accompanied by additional practice to help it sink in.'

Overall, the message was clear. Trainees felt there wasn't enough time to develop and reflect upon their teaching skills in a non-assessed, non-threatening environment. We decided to redesign our eight-week part-time CELTA timetable to take account of these concerns. Outlined below is a summary of what we did:

- Two weeks of input before any TP with plenty of opportunities for micro-teaching.
- Input and TP organised on a block basis. The two weeks of input outlined above was followed by a week of TP.
- A focused programme of unobserved TP. The planning of these sessions was given the same priority as assessed lessons.
- Input sessions which 'reacted' to issues arising from the previous week's block of TP. The focus of these sessions was based on trainees' requests.
- Tutorials were extended to a maximum of 30 minutes each.

So what effect did these changes have? Well, trainees were extremely positive about micro-teaching, the formalised programme of unobserved TP and 'reactive' input. Some candidates indicated, however, that they would have preferred an opportunity to teach each week rather than doing TP in blocks. For the trainer, the course felt less stressful, TP student numbers remained consistent throughout despite the new timetable, and the standard of teaching was generally high. Of course, this could have had nothing to do with the changes we had made! Overall reaction to our presentation at IATEFL was positive and thought-provoking. Clearly it would be difficult to use the block system on a four-week intensive CELTA course and some trainers wondered what effect our timetable might have on TP students' attendance in their particular context. However, it's a timetable that we would use again with some slight modifications.

For a longer version of this article please contact the authors at the e-mail address below.

E-mail: nick1009@hotmail.com

4.9 Overcoming the technological barrier: Teachers and computers can be allies

Valéria Siniscalchi *Rio de Janeiro State University, Brazil*

Can we talk about an 'IT enthusiasm'? Is technology always welcome? It is quite evident that for a great number of teachers technology represents a threat. Besides the several roles teachers have always had in the classroom, they now feel under pressure to be 'modern' and to develop computer skills, which most of the time represents an extra burden. Having worked as a teacher trainer for 20 years, I sympathise with these teachers and believe that the sooner EFL teachers can be helped with computer skills, the better. This was the reason why I decided to develop a training project at the English Language and Literatures Undergraduate Course of the Rio de Janeiro State University in Brazil, devising activities that were integrated into the curriculum and which aimed at developing future EFL teachers' technological skills.

Apart from technical problems, the main difficulties teachers usually have include pressure from society, institutions and students to use technology; inadequate training; and the wealth of information on the Internet updated at a speed no human being can cope with. This means teachers have to develop special skills to find, select, evaluate and process information in new ways. However, computers have become part of our lives, and educators cannot fall behind. Students use computers in their lives and expect schools to do the same. Moreover, as communication in a globalised world has become a real purpose for learning English, teachers have an opportunity they should not miss: using the Internet as a motivational tool and as authentic linguistic input.

The project involved activities carried out in a computer lab, which were related to the content of the different courses of the undergraduate programme. The activities aimed at the practice of the English language, familiarisation with the technological tools and the development of computer skills for students' personal and future professional use. The activities were grouped in three main areas: the computer seen as a tool, as a means of communication and/or as a source of information and practice.

As examples of group one, we may cite the organisation of an online campaign to advertise a seminar at the university (4th term) and the preparation of a Powerpoint Presentation (2nd term). Group two included an activity to evaluate Web pages and create one for the class (4th term) and a class chat organized by the teacher, which was then printed and analysed (1st term). In group three, students could look at online synopses of TV programmes to practise narratives and summaries (5th term) or compare online newspapers (6th term).

These were only a few examples of an integrated technological training programme that can be offered as part of pre-service EFL teacher education. University students can benefit from activities which try to make use of the computer to facilitate and enrich processes, to stimulate creativity, to access information and promote communication with the world.

E-mail: valerias@ism.com.br

4.10 Virtual discussion in distance language teacher education: Time well spent?

Martin Wedell *University of Leeds, England*

(Italics indicate quotes from interviews with learners)

Master's level language teacher development programmes expose participants to multiple points of view, usually with an ultimate aim of encouraging them to critically assess the relevance of different viewpoints to their own contexts, thereby hopefully developing new understandings, which may in turn lead to new professional beliefs and behaviours.

Discussion, implying interaction and participation, is an important part of this process. For distance learners, working in isolation, attempts are frequently made to provide opportunities for such discussion 'virtually', online, in order to enable:

- critical consideration of multiple perspectives arising from topics discussed, hopefully contributing to professional development as outlined above
- development of relationships between learners, and lessening of their feelings of existing only in some distant 'cyberia' (Muirhead, B. http://www.ifets.ieee.org/discussions/discuss_january2001.html accessed 05/02/02)

To provide such opportunities on a distance MEd TESOL, tutors designed materials with each unit containing up to six tasks, which learners were asked to complete by posting responses to asynchronous discussion rooms within the programme website.

Technically, this worked well. Learners completed most tasks and read each other's postings. Interviews with learners during their Leeds summer school indicated that the discussion room had lessened isolation and helped them manage their work. In terms of learning, they reported that others' responses had *helped me clarify my thoughts* and had *shone light on views and concepts I had not thought of before*. The process of having to put thoughts into words had *crystallised things*, and having to *sound out ideas* had been useful. There was, however, little interaction.

Reasons given included:

- Insufficient time: *Because of other commitments we are rushing through the units with our own answers. We have little time to read the others' responses and react to them.*
- Variable quality of responses. *I enjoyed reading GD's* (English MT) *submissions, the others were working in the L2. I don't think I'd be able to do it in Chinese.*
- No evaluation. *If it was evaluated, we would be more aware and more careful.*

Does lack of interaction matter? *I feel everyone is writing for him/herself and the posting only has significance for the writer.* If we believe that learning involves critically considering varied viewpoints, this comment suggests that our 'discussion' does not effectively encourage this.

Some/all of the following may encourage greater interaction:

Decrease variability of response quality

- Pair/group learners to work on tasks together to try to lessen language-related effects.

Tighter task management by tutors

- Have one core task per unit
- Specify one week each unit during which the task must be completed (and a question posed to other learners)
- During the following week each learner/pair/group must do one of the following:
  - respond to a question that interests them
  - comment on one other response
  - provide a summary of responses for others to comment on.

More careful task focus

- Conceptual understandings/interpretations rather than factual descriptions/narratives to generate more varied responses likely to engender discussion

Evaluation

- Develop assessment criteria for participation in online discussion.
- Make appropriate references to online discussions one of the criteria for assignment marking.

E-mail: M.Wedell@education.leeds.ac.uk

4.11 Training online tutors

Nicky Hockly *Fundación Universitaria Iberoamericana, Barcelona, Spain*

An increasing number of institutions offer online courses for both students and teachers in the field of EFL, ranging from language courses for EFL students to MAs in Linguistics or TESOL. However, the demands placed on an online tutor are different to those placed on face-to-face teachers, whether they be language teachers or MA instructors. Tutors are typically offered very little training in the skills necessary for encouraging learning in an online environment.

This talk explored some of the issues involved in online tutoring, and looked closely at how tutors can be trained in specific online tutoring skills, such as e-moderation, negotiation, climate-setting, and evaluating online participation. These issues were examined in the light of a number of online training courses which I have run, and examples of trainee-tutor participation and interaction were presented from my own data.

A model online tutor training course, based on five stages (see Salmon *E-Moderating: The Key to Teaching and Learning Online* Kogan Page 2000), was discussed, with tutor skills needed for each stage. Examples of tutor participation in past courses were given, and ideas for online tasks types for various skills were presented.

Below is a summary of the stages and skills:

Stage 1: Access and climate setting

The most important thing when starting an online tutor training course is that trainee tutors learn to use the learning platform effectively – a number of introductory tasks which require trainees to use the system and at the same time to get to know co-trainees, is used to do this. Tutors also need to reflect on these introductory activities, so as to be competent in setting up similar activities on their own courses. Encouraging participation is another skill focused on at this first stage, and various examples of tutor messages to reluctant students are analysed and discussed.

Stage 2: Social skills

Here trainee tutors focus on the skills of motivating and supporting participants, the issue of 'lurking'[1] is explored, and online student expectations are discussed. Research has shown that the majority of dropouts on courses are caused (apart from by external causes such as illness, etc.) by a mismatch between student expectations and the reality of the course. Trainee tutors also create a number of protocols (e.g. for chats and asynchronous online discussions), and dealing with 'problem' areas is explored.

Stage 3: Dealing with knowledge and content

Skills examined at this stage of the course are:

- Weaving responses and summarising asynchronous discussions.
- Listening, questioning, negotiating and feeding back to student input, both synchronous and asynchronous.

- Encouraging knowledge construction, for example through carefully set up online jigsaw tasks.

Stage 4: Development and reflection

At this final stage of the course, we examine the importance of setting clear outcomes for our students. Overt reflection, by both tutor and tutor-trainee, on the learning process during the course is emphasised – for this, individual tutor-trainee online reflective journals (which have been in operation from the beginning of the course), are shared and discussed.

Finally, evaluation procedures for online courses are highlighted.

E-mail: nicky@funiber.org

Editor's note

1 'Lurking' refers to the practice of a member of an e-group reading the group's postings on a regular basis, but posting occasionally or not at all. It is not a pejorative term. Lurking is recommended for beginners who need to learn the history and practices of the group before posting.

4.12 Should there be concern as TESOL distance programmes multiply?

Brian Winn-Smith *Eurolink Courses, England*

With the number of Internet users approaching 500 million and the continuing growth of ELT, it is not surprising that TESOL distance courses continue to mushroom. The demand worldwide for English and teachers of English continues unabated.

Given the recent growth of TESOL distance programmes, there is a real need for quality control, and in some cases protection for new entrants to the profession.

In addition to those face-to-face and hybrid courses leading to UCLES, Trinity College, the College of Teachers and some recognised university qualifications, thanks to the Internet, there is also a bewildering range of TESOL distance training courses currently on offer.

In the case of Diploma and Master's level programmes, few problems exist, since prospective clients are already pretty knowledgeable and able to find a course suited to their needs. In the case of new entrants to the profession, it is an entirely different matter. Most simply do not know what they should be looking for and may easily be misled. At present, little help or guidance is at hand.

Clearly, TESOL distance programmes are here to stay, and their continued growth is certain. Ignored by so many for so long, appropriate accreditation in this field is clearly essential. As to why, let us consider just one instance. No quality assurance scheme was built into the recent UK government ILA[1] funding scheme, resulting in thousands of disappointed clients and losses of millions of pounds. The only criteria that the learning provider had to offer the contractor to gain access to government money were a name, address and telephone number, and details of the bank account where the cash was to be sent. No other validation whatever was required.

'Is it accredited?' This is probably the most frequently asked, and to some extent the most misunderstood, question regarding TEFL/TESOL distance education courses. Who passes judgement on the legitimacy of a distance TESOL certificate or diploma? Quite simply, the schools or institutions around the world that employ English language teachers. Accreditation is the tool that can help school owners and Directors of Studies make employment decisions. If a programme is accredited by an internationally recognised body, even though methods of delivery may well be different, the school can be certain not just about course quality assurance, but also about such elements as syllabus content, course process, level and depth of coverage.

The anonymity of cyberspace can provide ideal camouflage for hole-in-the-wall operators offering non-accredited distance ELT programmes that are a disservice to the profession.

The workshop set out to consider and attempt to measure specific aspects of quality assurance in the case of sixteen TESOL distance programme providers selected at random from the World Wide Web. Further details can be obtained from the author at the e-mail address below.

E-mail: brian@eurolinkcourses.co.uk

Editor's note

1 The ILA (Individual Learning Account) was a government funding programme launched in September 2000 to help people in work pay for learning and personal development. By October 2001 2.5 million members were registered as eligible to undertake subsidised learning and some 9,000 organisations were registered as learning providers. However, due to evidence of abuse by a small minority of providers, the programme was shut down in December 2001.

5 INSTRUCTIONAL APPROACHES

5.1 Task-based instruction: Theory, research, practice

Peter Skehan *King's College, London*

Introduction

Second language acquisition researchers originally drew their inspiration from the massive change that took place in first language acquisition research during the 1960s. Early work suggested that the same inexorable processes that occur with the learning of one's first language might be operative (Dulay & Burt 1974) in the second language case, and led to the conclusion that duplicating the conditions of first language acquisition would lead to successful second language acquisition. Krashen (1985), for example, proposed the Input Hypothesis to account for this fundamental similarity of the learning that takes place in both contexts, and Long (1983), in early versions of his interaction hypothesis, also implied that structured pedagogic intervention is the wrong approach to take (see also Long & Crookes 1991). Instead, he proposed that interaction itself is sufficient to drive forward development and that giving learners the right sort of tasks to do is the ideal way to promote such interaction.

These early views of second language acquisition soon ran into trouble. Evidence mounted that there is a critical period for language acquisition (DeKeyser 2000), indicating that first and second language acquisition are not the same, and the hard-wired advantages possessed by the child are no longer available to the second language learner. Worse, educational research also proved negative. Immersion education in Canada, for example, contains large amounts of input for learners, but this input is not associated with native-like capacities to *produce* language (Harley & Swain 1984). As a result, a significant view currently within second language acquisition research is that providing learners with comprehensible input, or interaction opportunities, may not be enough to assure development.

In addition, there is a need for some degree of focus-on-form, i.e. within communicative activities, a need to make prominent the formal dimension of language (Long & Robinson 1998; Doughty & Williams 1998b). Otherwise, learners will engage in communication, but concern themselves more with getting the communicative activity or task done, through the use of comprehension and production strategies, thus bypassing form. Indeed, learners may, in the interests of task fulfilment, come to rely excessively upon strategies of communication and so make continued progress in developing an interlanguage system more difficult (Skehan 1998).

We can also distinguish between strong and weak forms of task-based instruction. A strong form of the communicative approach, or more properly, a task-based approach, does not generally lead to pre-selection of forms. Learners are given communicative things to do, and then use whatever language seems appropriate. The main pedagogic challenge in this situation concerns how learners are supported not to forget form. It is assumed that pre-selecting structures, and choosing tasks which make use of pre-selected structures will be ineffective, and not allow acquisition to proceed. But simply to require meanings to be transacted would run the risk, noted above, that there will not be continued progress. As a result, the strong form of the task-based approach has to incorporate pedagogic strategies to enable whatever language is needed to transact the task to then be capitalised upon. Conversely, the weak form does enable pre-selection of structures, and then attempts to find satisfactory tasks which do not lose communicative qualities while still allowing structural focus. We will return to this opposition later.

At this point it is also worth discussing the nature of performance, and exploring complexity, accuracy and fluency. Task-based research has shown each of these to be distinct from one another (Skehan & Foster 1997; 2001), and even to be in competition. It has also been proposed that they represent different stages of the learning process. This starts with development in the underlying interlanguage system, i.e. greater complexity, as learners attempt to use more advanced language and re-structure what they know of the target language. Then there is the reduction of error, as learners try to achieve control over the new language sub-systems, and to use them correctly. Finally there is the stage where the particular part of the interlanguage system can also be produced in real time, without undue pausing or interruption, i.e. the level of control becomes even more advanced and native-like.

The performance and the development-oriented interpretations of complexity, accuracy and fluency can be related to one another. First, task characteristics and task conditions can prioritise new language and risk taking; on other occasions they can predispose conservatism and error avoidance; and on others push learners to gain fluent control over aspects of the target language which are becoming more easily used. The first two of these areas concern form, while the last, fluency, is more concerned with expressing meaning, in real time. As we will see below, much task research explores these three performance areas, and their connections with development. If the performance areas which are appropriate for a learner's current developmental profile are fostered through careful task choice, more balanced development will occur, and excessive reliance on one performance area, e.g. fluency, will be avoided, i.e. learners are less likely to become dependent on lexically-based production strategies. In this way, guided current performance can support longer-term change and *development*.

Task-based instruction: A review of research findings

There have been a large number of research studies published in the last decade which have advanced our understanding of task use considerably. These studies have explored how different task features impact upon performance, and how the conditions under which tasks are done influence the language which is produced. Regarding task features, the research suggests the following findings:

Task characteristic	Influence upon performance
• structured tasks	clearly greater fluency, tendency towards greater accuracy
• familiar information	greater fluency and greater accuracy
• outcomes requiring justifications	markedly greater complexity of language
• interactive vs. monologic tasks	interactive tasks produce markedly more accuracy and complexity, monologic tasks more fluency

The first characteristic, structured tasks, concerns tasks which have a clear macrostructure, often involving a clear time sequence, e.g. explain to someone how to get to your home to turn off an oven which has been left on (Foster & Skehan 1996); or retell the Mr Bean video where Mr Bean goes to a restaurant (Skehan & Foster 1999), a situation and story which have a predictable sequence of actions. Familiar tasks are those where the information simply needs to be retrieved from organised memory by the person doing the task, as opposed to tasks which require retrieval and manipulation of information. Outcomes requiring justifications are illustrated by two decision-making tasks (see Foster & Skehan 1996, and Skehan & Foster 1997). In the first, learners, in pairs, had to agree on judicial sentences appropriate to a series of crimes. In the second, again in pairs, learners had to agree on the advice appropriate to the writers of letters to a magazine agony aunt. In the first of these tasks, opinions only had to be justified to agree on the number of years someone would go to jail, and learners did this in a rather superficial manner. In the second, a simple numerical outcome was not possible, and learners had to justify their advice, which provoked much greater language complexity. Finally, a consistent finding in task research has been that when learners work together interactively, other things being equal, they produce more advanced *and* more accurate language, but this language is produced less fluently, with more pausing, and with greater amounts of reformulation, repetition and false starts. Monologic tasks, such as narrative retellings, produce greater fluency, but lower accuracy and complexity. (Interestingly and somewhat ironically, it is narratives that are the staple format used by those who design oral assessment procedures – in other words, they may be biasing performance for the worse!)

These findings suggest that the choice of task that a teacher makes is not neutral, and that to choose a particular task type may well support some areas of language performance and disadvantage others. Some tasks tend to produce more complex language, others greater accuracy, while others favour fluency. Given that complexity represents the 'cutting edge' in language, where development occurs, while accuracy and fluency are more concerned with greater control, a teacher's choice of tasks will not simply influence ongoing performance, but will also have implications for change over the longer term.

There have also been a number of studies into the effects of varying the conditions under which tasks are done. Two major areas have received attention in this regard: the effects of pre-task planning, and the effects of post-task activities. Regarding planning, it has been shown in a number of studies (Crookes 1989; Foster & Skehan 1996; Wigglesworth 1997; Mehnert 1998, Ortega 1999) that giving learners the opportunity to plan before a task consistently produces greater complexity of language and greater fluency. These effects are strong and dependable, and imply that if one wants learners to draw upon more advanced language, and if one wants them to use this language with less hesitation and pausing, giving planning time is essential. Interestingly, it appears that giving learners time to plan by themselves is more effective than having them plan in groups, but that each of these is less effective than the teacher being involved in the planning process (Foster & Skehan 1999).

Researching the post-task phase has also been rewarding, and has figured prominently in research I have done with Pauline Foster. An example of post-task activities is informing learners before they do a task that some of them will be required to re-do the task subsequently in front of the entire class. The justification for this is that the 'threat' of a future public performance will induce learners, while doing the task, to try to be more accurate, because they see the connection between the task and how well they will do later, when standards of correctness may be more obvious. Further, the future task will not compromise the naturalness and communicativeness of the actual task, since the teacher will not be present at the task stage. An alternative post-task condition (attempting to achieve the same result of greater accuracy) would be to record learner performance during a task (which is done anyway during research studies), and then give the tape to learners so that they have to transcribe some of their own performance. Once again, the intention is to focus learners' attention on form, since they will be paying close attention to what they themselves have said. Skehan and Foster (1997) made the prediction that accuracy, selectively, would be advantaged in a post-task condition. In two studies, (Skehan & Foster 1997, Skehan & Foster, ms) this prediction for a post-task effect upon accuracy was confirmed, but only for interactive tasks. There was a higher level of accuracy with personal information exchange and narrative tasks, but this did not reach statistical significance. In addition, there was a significant practice effect: as time went on in the study, over two to three weeks, the effect on accuracy grew in strength.

It became clear in our research that the role of interaction is complex and productive in task-based performance. Interactive tasks lead to more complexity and accuracy of language, and the post-task conditions we used only worked (in the sense of reaching statistical significance for the accuracy scores) when used with interactive tasks. These results led us to wonder what particular qualities of interaction push for more interesting use of form in language.

In this respect, four fairly distinct possibilities present themselves. One can hypothesise that:

- interaction simply gives learners more time to plan while doing a task, since there will be periods when their interlocutor is speaking, and so although attention is necessary to some degree (or has to be feigned!), the learner can give some time to planning her own performance;
- interaction provides greater opportunity for the negotiation of meaning (Long & Robinson 1998), such that conversational breakdowns lead to repair and the incorporation of feedback provided during such repair;
- interaction pushes learners to be more precise in their speech. They want to be understood, and their interlocutor is present (in contrast to the imagined interlocutor in most narrative tasks), so they may focus on the detail of their language to make sure they are comprehensible;
- interaction enables learners to scaffold one another, i.e. two learners, if engaged in successful interaction, in effect provide one another with useful language which can be recycled, either because it is interestingly complex or because it is recognised to be accurate.

Using these possibilities, we went back to our data, and re-coded it to see if we could capture the quality of the interaction in such a way that this would correlate with how accurately learners used language while doing the task. We coded learner performance for negotiation of meaning; for length of time spent talking (by the interlocutor as well as the speaker); and for what we can term 'engagement', i.e. the extent to which learners accepted one another's contributions, didn't try to dominate, and instead 'built' the conversation collaboratively. When we did this, it is the engagement dimension of interaction which correlated with accuracy. Learners who validate one another's conversational contributions, and expand them, tend to produce language which is both more accurate and more complex. This promising result, obtained by exploiting some already existing data for re-analysis, is exciting. We next plan to design new studies and collect data specifically to address this issue.

Once again research findings are relevant for teacher decision-making. They indicate how changes in performance can result from what happens before and after the task itself. The research findings are, therefore, relevant for teachers planning how they are going to implement tasks in their classrooms.

Putting task research in pedagogic context

Researchers, or at least, quantitatively oriented researchers, inevitably focus: they try to control and isolate influences which can be shown to have an impact upon performance. Hence the focus on task characteristics (even though it may not be entirely natural to 'decompose' tasks in this way). Only in this way can the impact of particular task characteristics be revealed clearly. Similarly, the focus on task conditions: the previous section has reviewed the effects of pre-task planning and post-task accuracy-promoting activities.

But it is important to point out that pre-task work is not limited to planning, nor is post-task work only possible if it promotes accuracy. In fact, it is useful to broaden each of these stages, pre- and post-task, to explore what wider potential each contains, and also how they can contribute to language development. The pre-task phase is essentially concerned with preparing learners to do tasks in a more effective manner. Planning, as we have seen, leads to greater complexity and greater fluency. In the first case here, the planning seems connected with learners reinterpreting tasks and raising their level of ambition. This pushes them to need more complex language as they see greater potential in the task to express worthwhile meanings. The fluency effect, in contrast, seems to be concerned with rehearsal: learners assemble useful language, and so when the task is being done, they are able to access material in a more effective manner.

Other pre-task alternatives may achieve slightly different effects. For example, learners could be given a pre-task task to do, as in Prabhu's work (1987), where the pre-task, in effect, organises learners' thinking for the task to come. This, too, would be expected to lead to greater fluency, and also perhaps greater accuracy, as learners are given a structure for the task they are going to do. This is particularly likely to happen if the pre-task is not simply working with relevant input of some form, but goes further and acts as a rehearsal for what is going to come. One could anticipate even greater accuracy in this case. And, of course, there are also possibilities of training and teaching learners pre-task, with the idea that language is made salient because of the coverage within the training or teaching materials.

In some ways, though, it is the post-task phase which has been least exploited and which contains the greatest potential. The research studies mentioned earlier tried to achieve a sort of Machiavellian manipulation of learner attention, so that accuracy during the task becomes more highly prioritised. Post-task work can have some other general aims, including provision of feedback; analysis and consciousness-raising; and consolidation.

Tasks, if they work well, will engage learners, and create a need to mean. In an idealised interpretation, we can hope that doing a task will push learners to incorporate useful and emerging language, as well as to use language for performance in real time. If this happened, all our problems would be solved! But clearly some of the time, all a task will do is make salient some aspect of the language system, but without giving it a sense of closure or complete learning. During the task, for example, a learner may notice some useful language in what the interlocutor says. Alternatively, a learner may want to say something, and realise that there is a gap (Swain 1995) in their interlanguage system (in which case, either the learner abandons, improvises, or is helped by the other learner(s)). It is also possible that doing the task will push the learner to notice some connection in the language system which wasn't apparent before, as, for example, when a different means for saying the same thing is noticed (e.g. modal verbs instead of 'it is possible'). In all these cases, a good task, in addition to being interesting in itself, is likely to leave a 'rich residue'. One of the functions of the post-task phase is then to capitalise upon what has been made salient in this way, and to take it further. In other words, the task is likely to have produced in the learner a considerable readiness to learn and sensitivity to form. This is what has to be responded to: not to do so could be very frustrating for the learner.

Feedback, at this stage, would consist of the teacher responding to learner requests regarding language which has come up in the task but which the learner feels has been used incorrectly, or is simply not currently understood. The teacher can respond to this highly salient language at exactly the most propitious moment. (If task performance is recorded, provision of feedback in this way could be even more facilitated.) Analysis (which in a sense is elaborate feedback) would consist of teacher help so that learners could realise how specific examples of language which have come up in a task fit into a larger system, rather than being isolated elements. Learners, for example, may have noticed that different forms of future time reference have been used. The teacher can exploit this to talk about the different structures (in English in this case) that can be used to refer to the future. Feedback and analysis presuppose that it is some sort of problem that is motivating the post-task phase. But a final option does not assume a problem. Instead, it focuses on the way what has been transient and fleeting in the task may need to be consolidated and 'fixed' by more extensive treatment. It is difficult, mid-task, to attend to form and retain it. There is scope, therefore, for the post-task phase to provide more extended treatment of a particular area which has come up during task work, and to devise methods of working on the area, providing practice, and using sustained focus. The overriding purpose is simply to consolidate, so that it is more likely that a form will be used effectively in the future.

These claims can be most effectively illustrated by discussing two proposals which have been made for pedagogic frameworks within which teachers can use tasks: those of Virginia Samuda (2001) and Jane Willis (1996). In effect, these represent the weak and strong forms of a task-based approach which were mentioned earlier – to 'finesse' particular structures, in the former case, or to accept whatever emerges, in the latter. Samuda proposes a (long) class-oriented sequence which follows the stages (a) input data, (b) operations on input data, and (c) consolidation and reflection (i.e. pre-task, task, and post-task, in the terms discussed in this article). In addition, she distinguishes between knowledge-constructing tasks, i.e. tasks intended to push learners to develop new forms, and knowledge-activating tasks, i.e. tasks which promote salience, so that learners are more likely to mobilise language which they already know, but may not be so likely to use.

An example of a knowledge-constructing task is what Samuda terms the 'things in pockets' task. Learners are provided with some objects supposedly found in the pocket of a coat left in a plane. They are also provided with a matrix linking the objects with degrees of probability regarding the owner of the coat, and this constitutes the input data. Their task is to speculate on the identity of the owner of the coat on the basis of these possessions. The task targets modality, both at a simple level ('maybe', 'perhaps'), a slightly less elementary level ('it is possible'), and then the main focus for the task, the use of modal verbs. Learners are given such a focussed task because it creates an extended period in which a 'need to mean' has been contrived, and in which, as learners work on the task, the teacher can work with them, and introduce new forms, to attempt to induce the learners to allow these particular new forms to supplant more restricted methods of expressing modality. The task is completed with learners making a report, in the form of a poster, such that there is opportunity for consolidation and reflection on the forms which have just been introduced.

There are several points of connection between this practical approach and the earlier analyses of tasks. First, rather than planning, the methodology uses a pre-task (or perhaps an orienting task), which organises and structures the information the learners will use during the task. Second, the teacher's role during the task itself is to 'lead from behind', i.e. to attempt to use the ways learners are engaging with the task and expressing meanings to provide relevant assistance with language form when learners themselves have created a 'need to mean'. In other words, the classroom methodology structures the way in which learners are induced to notice a gap in output (Swain 1995), and then the teacher supplies language relevant to the gap which has just been made salient. Third, the final phase requires learners to revisit the task so that their work can be communicated to others. In order to produce a report (in the form of a poster), they are drawn into reworking and consolidating, so that what they have learned about modality is publicly presented, and will receive considerable attention to form as learners try to avoid producing posters containing mistakes.

A contrasting approach to using tasks is advocated by Willis (1996), who proposes the following pedagogic sequence:

Pre-task

- introduction to the topic and task
- exposure to real language (tape recordings of native speakers completing the same task
- use of texts and activities upon those texts

Task cycle
- task
- planning
- drafting and rehearsal
- teacher assistance with language
- report

Language focus
- analysis
- practice

There are similarities and differences here with the approach advocated by Samuda (2001). The most striking difference is that this methodology for using tasks does not imply any pre-selection of form. It is intended to make salient whatever language learners see as relevant. Although the pre-task may have an impact on what language learners perceive as relevant, essentially the role of the teacher is to react to whatever language emerges as important, and then help learners to address the gap which has been noted. It is also striking that for Willis, planning follows rather than precedes the task. More properly, planning precedes the report phase, i.e. the phase by which learners should have done something about any gaps which have been noticed, and should be trying to mobilise resources so that the report phase is completed in a manner significantly better than the original task. So we can see in this methodology a pre-task phase, a task phase, and then a post-task phase (even though Willis herself locates the report as being within the task itself). Further, this report corresponds to Samuda's report, which is in that scheme the final phase, and is oriented towards consolidation.

It is only after the report phase in Willis' sequence that the lesson switches to an overt language focus. In other words, Willis proposes two distinct post-task phases, one for consolidation, and then the second for extension. By this second post-task phase, in other words, the focus on language will have been 'earned' and made salient by all the preceding activity, and so integration of new forms into an existing interlanguage structure can be accomplished more effectively. The approach, essentially, is consistent with Swain's (1995) proposals to encourage learners to 'notice the gap'. What is most important in Willis' approach is (a) input materials push learners into 'primed' areas, (b) learners are given considerable support by the teacher *after* they have noticed whatever gap may have emerged, and (c) language analysis, systematisation and consolidation take place *after* there has been some interlanguage restructuring.

Conclusion

This paper started from theory and research, and then moved towards more practical proposals. It is worth restating some of the arguments, since the point of the paper is to argue that these two perspectives need to work together if they are to work effectively.

From theory, the main insight is that a focus on form is necessary within a task-based approach to instruction. If such a focus is not present, there is a danger that learners will become effective at transacting tasks, but not pressure their language systems to change, and not have sufficient concern to eliminate error. Form and meaning will not, in other words, come together effectively. From research, we have seen that a range of findings are now available, regarding the predictable effects of certain characteristics and the predictable effects of pre- and post-task activities. (We have also seen that what has been researched is only a subset of what might have been researched in each of these areas: there is a great deal still to be done.)

There have been a number of critiques of tasks in the last few years. For example, Bruton (2002) has recently argued that tasks should know their place, and be used as the final (and relatively minor) phase in the conventional '3 Ps' approach, of presentation, practice, production. Part of the argument made in critiques of this sort (see also Seedhouse 1997, 1999) is that tasks have not been proven to be effective. The points made in the last paragraph, though, suggest that it is premature to dismiss tasks in this way. The length of time that tasks have been researched systematically is not great. Research is showing promise already, even if the findings are massively incomplete. We can expect more and more useful findings to emerge in the near future. Above all, though, what task theory and research have already established is that although there are dangers in using tasks, there are also opportunities, since we are learning more and more about pedagogic decisions which can be made to minimise these dangers. As Dylan Thomas said, nothing in life is simple. What we are learning is how to achieve the potential of tasks, while avoiding the pitfalls.

What we have seen in the practical approaches with tasks (cf. Samuda & Willis) is that practitioners can explore methods of implementing tasks which make sense to teachers, and which are operable in classrooms. Undoubtedly, task research will continue, and will continue to establish findings relevant to choosing and using tasks. But this needs to be supplemented by more investigations which go beyond research settings, and which try to explore the viability of implementing many of the emerging findings in realistic contexts. Only in this way will we learn whether the claims which researchers make are sufficiently robust to be relevant for classrooms.

Bibliography

Bruton, A. (2002) From tasking purposes to purposing tasks. In *English Language Teaching Journal*, 56, 3, 280–288.

Bygate, M., P. Skehan & M. Swain (Eds.) (2001) *Researching Pedagogic Tasks: Second Language Learning, Teaching, and Testing*. London: Longman.

Crookes, G. (1989) Planning and interlanguage variation. In *Studies in Second Language Acquisition*, 11: 367–383.

DeKeyser, R. (2000) The robustness of critical period effects in second language acquisition. In *Studies in Second Language Acquisition*, 22, 499–533.

Doughty, C. & J. Williams (1998a) *Focus on Form in Classroom Second Language Acquisition*, Cambridge: Cambridge University Press.

Doughty, C. & J. Williams (1998b) Pedagogic choices in focus on form. In Doughty C. & J. Williams (Eds.).

Dulay, H. & M. Burt (1974) Natural sequences in child second language acquisition. In *Language Learning*, 24, 37–53.

Foster, P. & P. Skehan (1996) The influence of planning on performance in task-based learning. In *Studies in Second Language Acquisition*, 18, 3, 299–324.

Foster, P. & P. Skehan. (1999) The effect of source of planning and focus of planning on task-based performance. In *Language Teaching Research*, 3,3, 185–214.

Harley, B. & M. Swain (1984) The interlanguage of immersion students and its implications for second language teaching. In Davies, A., C. Criper & A. Howatt (Eds.) *Interlanguage* 291–311. Edinburgh: Edinburgh University Press.

Krashen, S. (1985) *The Input Hypothesis*, London: Longman.

Long, M. (1983) Native speaker/non-native speaker conversation and the negotiation of comprehensible input. In *Applied Linguistics*, 4, 2, 126–141.

Long, M. & G. Crookes (1991) Three approaches to task-based syllabus design. In *TESOL Quarterly* 26, 1, 27–55.

Long, M. & P. Robinson (1998) Focus on form: theory, research, and practice. In Doughty, C. & J. Williams (Eds.), *Focus on form in classroom SLA*, Cambridge: CUP.

Mehnert, U. (1998) The effects of different lengths of time for planning on second language performance. In *Studies in Second Language Acquisition*, 20, 83-108

Ortega L. (1999) Planning and focus on form in L2 oral performance. In *Studies in Second Language Acquisition*, 21, 109–148.

Prabhu, N. S. (1987) *Second Language Pedagogy* Oxford: Oxford University Press.

Samuda, V. (2001) Guiding relationships between form and meaning during task performance: the role of the teacher. In Bygate, Skehan, & Swain (Eds.).

Seedhouse, P. (1997) Combining form and meaning. In *English Language Teaching Journal*, 51, 4, 336–344.

Seedhouse, P. (1999) Task-based interaction. In *English Language Teaching Journal* 53, 3, 149–156.

Skehan, P. (1998) *A Cognitive Approach to Language Learning*. Oxford: Oxford University Press.

Skehan, P. & P. Foster (1997) The influence of planning and post-task activities on accuracy and complexity in task based learning. In *Language Teaching Research,* 1, 3.

Skehan, P. & P. Foster (1999) The influence of task structure and processing conditions on narrative retellings. In *Language Learning*, 49, 1, 93–120.

Skehan, P. & P. Foster (2001) Cognition and tasks. In Robinson, P. (Ed.)

Skehan P. and Foster P. (ms) The effects of post-task activities on the accuracy of language during task performance. King's College, London.

Swain, M. (1995) Three functions of output in second language learning. In Cook, G. & B. Seidelhofer (Eds.) *Principle and Practice in Applied Linguistics*. Oxford: Oxford University Press, 245–256.

Wigglesworth, J. (1997) An investigation of planning time and proficiency level on oral test discourse. In *Language Testing*, 14, 1, 85–106.

Willis, J. (1996) *A Framework for Task-based Learning*. London: Longman.

5.2 A T.O.P.I.C.-driven framework for language lesson design

Derrin Kent *International House, Barcelona, Spain*

In *Brighton Conference Selections* (2001) my colleague, Karl Kaliski, wrote of ways in which we had been using Task-Based Learning (TBL) as the central teaching paradigm on pre-service teacher training courses. We both still feel very strongly that the quality of our courses has improved significantly as a result of this work.

One problem we were encountering, however, was how to provide a realistic balance between, on the one hand, the proactive syllabus demands made by a coursebook (and by the in-house testing and evaluation systems of most language schools) and on the other hand, the reactive form-focus principles encouraged by TBL methodologies. The

A TOPIC-driven strategy for language lesson design

	Key Concepts	Learner Roles	Teacher Roles
Task/Text	• Pre-task • Identify/Create a need • Model text (of task) • Text treated as a vehicle for information	• *Communicate: receptively/ productively* • *Noticing (& recording?) gaps*	Selecting texts/tasks; Generating interest; Animating production; Identifying errors/gaps/good examples; Facilitating comprehension of a text; etc.
Observe Form	• Text can be treated as a language object/'noticing' • Language as: Lexis/ Grammar/Vocabulary/ Discourse/Function/etc. • Exercises, drills and activities	• *Making Hypotheses* • *Noticing Form* • *Recording Form* • *Restricted Language Use*	Setting 'guided discovery' challenges; 'Spotlighting' form in context/co-text; Clarifying where required; Providing focus exercises/drills/activities; etc.
Prepare	• Accuracy and Complexity • Stretch output • Focus on Form	• *Preparing thematically (ideas)* • *Preparing linguistically (useful language)*	Animating; Acting as a language resource; Intervening to shape: Stretching for complexity + correcting for accuracy; monitoring and recording form; etc.
Interact	• Audience and Performance • Outcome: A reason to …	• *Communicating* • *Seeking to achieve a communicative outcome?* • *Experimenting with target language form?* • *Authentic Language Use*	Animating and directing; Participating; Possibly intervening (but not interrupting) to shape; monitoring and recording form; etc.
Conclude/ Clarify Form	• Feedback on Outcome • Reactive Focus on Form: errors, gaps and good examples	• *Noticing Form* • *Recording Form*	Drawing the topic to a close; 'Signposting'?; Drawing learners' attention to their output: errors, gaps & good examples; Providing focus exercises/drills/activities; etc.

lesson design framework I describe here is my attempt to reconcile proactive and reactive approaches to language focus. It is only one of several lesson design frameworks which trainees are exposed to on my courses.

Lessons in this framework are built around a topic area, a task and a text. These are established in the 'T' stage. In the 'O' stage, students can, if the teacher wishes, focus on a discrete item of language. During the 'P' stage, they have time and support as they think about how they will use this language while expressing their own meanings. In the 'I' stage, as in TBL, students are later seeking to complete the task. Meaning is the central drive, but they can also be encouraged to make meaningful use of the target language item as they speak or write. After reaching some communicative conclusion according to the meaningful outcome of the 'I', the teacher will deal with 'whatever other language comes up' in the 'C' stage at the end of the lesson. Another session on my course focuses on how to design a task which is likely to prompt use of a particular language item.

While I sympathise, to an extent, with Kumaravadivelu's call for an end to 'method', my experience on teacher training courses has shown me that trainees appreciate an easily understandable model or framework around which to build their lessons in the early stages of their teaching. It serves to 'scaffold' their initial forays into language lesson design.

In my talk I had participants engage in a T.O.P.I.C.-driven lesson in practice, interjecting along the way to discuss the principles behind the framework with the audience. The table opposite gives an overview of the framework.

E-mail: derrin@ureach.com

5.3 Pre-sessional placement tests – are they any use?

Kathryn Aston *University of Sheffield, England*

Rationale

Pressure on course directors and teachers to 'process' students quickly and effectively on the first day or two of a pre-sessional EAP course often means that the content and face validity of placement tests are sacrificed to the need for convenience and speed. Many universities use tests that do not assess the students' grasp of the academic skills and vocabulary that they will need on their subject courses. In addition, the traditional interview-style speaking test does not allow the teacher to see how the student will interact with others in the classroom.

Procedure

I began with a short discussion in groups on what teachers, course directors and students want from pre-sessional placement tests; the methods used; and common problems. In the feedback, it emerged that teachers and students wanted a valid and reliable test, with no need to move misplaced students later, whereas directors wanted the test to be quick, easy and cheap to administer and mark. Methods included both IELTS-style skills tests and discrete-item grammar and vocabulary tests. Problems arose in balancing validity and practicality.

I then presented the results of my research into how British universities currently place pre-sessional students. Forty-four universities were contacted, of which ten gave details of their placement tests. Most of these (eight) used a combination of an essay and a discrete-item grammar and/or vocabulary test (supplemented by reading, listening, and speaking components in roughly half of all cases). This format is supported by research done by John Morley at the University of Manchester, which showed that this was the most effective way to place intermediate students, and it is also the basis of my own test.

There followed a discussion in small groups as to what grammar and vocabulary EAP students need to learn. Although some of this is subject-specific, it was agreed that there are areas of language common to many academic disciplines, such as vocabulary relating to cause and effect, or the conditional structures used for hypothesising. None of the universities tested this kind of language in their placement tests, including the Chaplen Test used at Manchester University, although my test does.

Examples were given from both tests, and the session then moved on to consider what teachers look for in a student's performance in a speaking test and how these elements can be identified. Teachers look for fluency, a certain degree of accuracy, range, interactive skills, effective self-expression and good pronunciation. The last four of these are specifically assessed in my own group speaking test. Participants agreed that interviewing large numbers of students requires a great deal of time and space, and that it could be difficult to moderate. There was some disagreement as to whether group discussion tasks were a better alternative, mainly because it was felt that some students may lack the confidence to speak much in a group of possibly unfamiliar people, although one participant had successfully implemented this type of test at his own institution.

E-mail: k.j.aston@sheffield.ac.uk

5.4 Hidden resources in the lo-tech classroom

Charles Hadfield *South Devon College, England*

Most teachers of most students in most classrooms in most schools in most countries, particularly those in the so-called 'developing world', lack all but the most basic of physical resources. Teachers in these contexts who have been exposed, however briefly, to less rudimentary contexts in the 'developed' world often feel that 'hi-tech' resources will solve their problems. And teachers from the 'developed' industrialised countries often find it hard to imagine how to cope in less fortunate situations (trainers in the UK, VSO volunteers, etc.). While accepting that I run the risk of 'making a virtue of necessity', my experience over the last 25 years in both hi-tech and lo-tech teaching environments reinforces my firm belief that the key 'resource' in any classroom is that of the human brain, but that our common human qualities often remain hidden to both teachers and learners. I often wonder how my great-uncle, a village schoolteacher in Shropshire in the late 19th/early 20th century, coped without electricity etc. ... Was his situation so very different from an early 21st century teacher in, say, Madagascar ...?

To illustrate some of my thinking around these questions, I began my workshop with a cassette recording of a visualisation text. 'Unfortunately' there was 'no electricity', so I had to abandon the hi-tech equipment and use my own voice instead – my purpose in staging this 'problem' was to demonstrate how even the simplest equipment often lets us down, even in a 'hi-tech' environment, and that for most of the world's classrooms, particularly in the developing world, we really have to 'get back to basics' and accept the limitations.

I talked through three visualisations of contrasting classrooms in different countries and climates, and then pegged a large poster to the washing line I had strung across the room. My poster diagram showed the different kinds of 'hidden human resources' available on tap in every classroom: students' knowledge, their emotions, values, humour, creativity, imagination and the 'real world' surrounding us. In essence, the collective brainpower available is a very powerful, yet often 'hidden' resource.

I then demonstrated several simple teaching techniques based on some of these tangible and intangible resources:

- DRILLING WITH DICE – the use of dice to create random (thus creative) cues and responses across the classroom, amongst groups, between individuals
- DISCUSSING WITH DICE – using dice to force a 'creative tension', requiring each individual in a large class to be ready to speak, to the whole group or within subgroups
- USING REALIA (washing on line) to drill/create stories – making the most of limited physical resources to tap the imagination
- USING OBJECTS to drill/create stories
- USING PEBBLES – exploring the more abstract qualities of the surroundings (e.g. pebbles, sand) to create characters, settings, plots which can in turn provide the basis for grammatical or imaginative work ('to see the world in a grain of sand')
- USING PAPERBAG PUPPETS – how very simple everyday items (e.g. paper bags) can stand in for more complex resources in the 'hi-tech' world such as video cartoons or sets of books. Investment of student energy in creating their own personae to aid language work
- CREATING AND WRITING NEW PROVERBS – the problem of written work in classrooms where paper and pens cannot be taken for granted. How to develop writing skills in contexts which militate against literacy. Links to the problems of providing reading materials
- TURNING THE CLASSROOM INTO A TOWN – linking the limited scope of the classroom to the boundless world outside

The workshop used these ideas and stimuli as a starting point from which teachers can start to explore an even more 'basic' approach to solving the 'problem' of limited physical resources. The irony is that the unlimited potential of the human mind is often more 'hidden' in the 'hi-tech' developed world than in the less fortunate context of developing country classrooms, where imagination and creativity are perhaps closer to the surface.

E-mail: charjill@dircon.co.uk

5.5 Using Cuisenaire rods to visualize abstract concepts and generate language

Nicholas Dimakides *University of Jyväskylä, Finland*

Cuisenaire rods are highly versatile tools in language teaching. One way in which they can be used is to have students work together to create a visual of an abstract concept which is meaningful to them. This concept, for example 'learning', 'health', 'harmony', or 'freedom', can come from the students' own area of study, from their hobbies and interests, or from life in general. By creating a 'visual' with the rods, students in a sense create a 'text' which they jointly own and in which they can invest. In order to succeed in this task, students need to dig deep into their linguistic resources. This activity, which is particularly appropriate for tactile and visual learners, respects learners by acknowledging that they all have something valuable to contribute. Using a visual metaphor allows for creativity and provides an element of enjoyment, resulting in a rich, shared experience. This helps to build community, which in turn facilitates learning.

This activity is based on David Hawkins' (1967) 'I, Thou, and It' framework (see *The Informed Vision: Essays on learning and human nature*. NY: Agathorn Press 1974), in which the teacher is the 'I', the learner is the 'Thou', and the content is the 'It'. In this case, the abstract concept, the rods, the visual, and the definition together comprise the 'It' which engages learners to such a degree that they seem to forget they are speaking a foreign language.

In the workshop participants were asked to work in groups of four to create a visual of learning in order to arrive at a jointly agreed-upon definition, 'Learning is ...' Each group then presented their visual and definition to the other groups. Finally, participants had an opportunity to comment on the entire experience and to ask questions. By experiencing the activity themselves, participants discovered that Cuisenaire rods can be used in this manner across the disciplines and with different levels of learners to generate language and make meaning.

Procedure: In groups of three or four, students are asked to create a visual of an abstract concept from their field of study. Based on their visual they should then agree upon a definition of that concept, which they write on flipchart paper and pin up on the wall behind their visual. Students should be encouraged to arrive at their own negotiated definition rather than use a textbook definition. Each group presents their visual and definition to the whole class. If time permits, each presentation can be followed by a short discussion.

Time: 20–30 minutes for group work, 3–5 minutes for each group presentation

Skills: Speaking, Listening, Writing, Reading

Follow-up: Teacher could print out the definitions and give a copy to each student during the next class, then refer back to the student-generated definitions later on in the course. Students may be asked to extend their definition by writing a paragraph about the concept in question. They can then be given the opportunity to read and comment on each other's extended definitions. To place more emphasis on writing, students may be asked to write an essay using their extended definition as the introductory paragraph.

E-mail: dimakide@cc.jyu.fi

5.6 'Here is the news': Improved pronunciation through student recordings

Robin Walker *Escuela Universitaria de Turismo de Asturias, Spain*

Recent research into the phonology of English as a *lingua franca* has thrown unexpected light onto the pedagogical appropriateness of certain traditional pronunciation activities, whilst simultaneously generating proposals for new techniques. In this respect, Jenkins (*The Phonology of English as an International Language* OUP 2000) puts forward a strong case for harnessing the phenomenon of accommodation as a tool for improving pronunciation.

The major problem with this approach is that it can only be used effectively with multilingual groups, where the quest for understanding leads speakers to converge on intelligible pronunciation. By contrast, with monolingual groups, intelligibility is achieved by converging on the shared mother tongue, and thus diverging from English. Clearly, on the one hand, such groups need comprehensible, objective criteria to guide them towards improved pronunciation, and, on the other, practice involving activities that are meaningful, individualised and offer usable feedback. The talk presented the use of task-based student recordings as a tool for improving pronunciation that responds well to these requirements.

After first outlining the theoretical considerations and reviewing early work by the presenter with recordings, the second part of the talk described the simplest task the presenter currently uses (a telephone dialogue with a hotel reception), and demonstrated the sequence that leads to the students' completed, marked recording. Emphasis was placed on the need to clarify at the outset exactly which aspects of pronunciation were to be evaluated. Any practice will then focus exclusively on these. Equal emphasis was laid on the need to be absolutely true to the marking criteria agreed upon with students, and on the obligation to ignore mistakes lying beyond this framework. The normal outcome of such a policy – high levels of success and consequently high motivation – was also discussed. Too often still, pronunciation is judged by its global proximity to native-speaker norms, leading to poor marks for most students, and decreasing motivation.

The last part of the talk focused on a more complex task – the recording of a weather forecast. The audience was given the opportunity to examine worksheets, and thus see how the recording fitted into a longer sequence based on the weather, a sequence involving both vocabulary and grammar. By listening to a recording made by one of the presenter's students, the audience had the chance to 'mark' the work for errors in the areas of pausing and linking, the pronunciation focus of the task. Such marking provides individual students with feedback, at which point they are invited to repeat the recording taking the feedback into account. This strategy takes the concepts of individualised feedback and the opportunity to re-work drafts, and employs them to generate focused practice in selected aspects of pronunciation.

The talk ended with a brief review of surveys carried out among the presenter's students, the results of which revealed a high degree of acceptance of this approach, as well as clear indications of learners having made careful preparation, and sometimes repeated attempts, before the completion of each recording.

E-mail: rwalker@fade.es

5.7 Creating and processing academic lectures

Heidi Evans *Kwansei Gakuin University, Japan*

Students in university contexts who take content courses in English often struggle to understand the lectures and take effective notes. English teachers can prepare students for these challenges by creating authentic lectures designed to be comprehensible, yet still provide students with an authentic listening experience. This workshop focused on how to create content-based lectures and use effective pre- and post-listening activities to support lecture listening.

Developing a meaningful lecture requires interest in a topic, not expertise, and begins with considering programme goals, student needs and your own interests. Choose topics that build schemata for future coursework. Use newspapers, the Internet, and secondary education texts to maintain a file of information, articles and visual aids connected to the topic.

Making content comprehensible without compromising authenticity requires thoughtful planning. Give the audience an overview of the organisation of the lecture at the beginning, use transitions to show relationships between ideas, and show a variety of visual aids to allow students to process information more effectively. Use repetition and paraphrasing of key points and new vocabulary, pauses between ideas, and elaboration through examples and details. Finally, incorporate examples or scenarios that are connected to the students' lives to maintain their interest and help them remember the content.

A meaningful lecture listening and note-taking experience also depends on the ability of students to process and record the information in a logical and organised way. Teach listening and note-taking skills such as distinguishing between main idea and details, or using abbreviations, and use schema-building activities to prepare students for success. Pre-listening homework could include learning new vocabulary, answering questions about their own experiences and opinions connected to the topic, or predicting content. Providing support through another class – for example, having students read a text about the topic in a reading class, having a discussion about the topic in a speaking class, or researching and reporting on the topic in a writing class – allows students to recycle vocabulary and preview (or review) content. During lecture listening, give students a partial outline to complete, have them identify main ideas and details, or ask them to order information as they hear it in the lecture. After the lecture, check comprehension, using interactive and communicative processing activities, such as writing their own test questions, peer review of notes, consolidation of notes, or self-assessment of their own notes to enable them to review and confirm content, and reflect on their own listening and note-taking strategies.

Throughout the workshop, participants viewed materials currently in use in an EAP programme, as well as parts of original lectures (on video) about environmental topics, and had opportunities to discuss how academic lectures could be used in their teaching situations. As more students choose content courses in English or move on to tertiary degrees, teachers need to broaden their expertise in materials development. Creating customised, comprehensible, lectures will allow teachers to more effectively prepare students for academic success.

E-mail: heidi@ksc.kwansei.ac.jp

5.8 Getting down to business: Engaging students through innovative project designs

Cynthia Quinn *Kwansei Gakuin University, Japan*

In Business English courses designed for pre-experience learners, teachers must find ways for students to 'connect' with business content by successfully appealing to students' interests. Project learning opportunities can create such a 'connection', as long as motivated participation remains high and group dynamics are successful. This summary introduces three general project 'components' that focus on sustaining learner involvement, promoting meaningful learning of business content and fostering smooth group relations. Engaged in a Business English course for Japanese policy studies undergraduates, students completed a series of three 'mini-projects': a stock portfolio project, a business trends project and a marketing project in which students created a new product and devised a marketing plan to support its introduction to the marketplace.

1 Roles and responsibility framework

Designating project leaders to assign responsibility and manage group work processes gives students an opportunity to experience 'team' dynamics typical of workplace settings. To illustrate how student leadership and membership roles can be solidified and effectively executed at the task level, the presenter showed examples such as a Roles Assignment Report, which clarifies leader and member responsibilities and expectations, as well as a Project Update assignment, or regular class discussions, in which leaders inform the class of project development decisions and seek feedback on their ideas. Overall, this framework fosters efficiency and helps maintain equitable participation.

2 Emphasis on meaningful content

Making content relevant to students' interests can be accomplished in a variety of ways, one of which is to promote learner discovery of business interests and topic preferences. The pre-experience learner, however, can be easily daunted by such freedom. When grappling with unfamiliar business content, students need support, so it is essential for the teacher to effectively guide student efforts to personalise content during the *early* stages of project development. In the talk, several tasks were suggested that aid learner discovery, many of which derive from an assortment of primary research assignments.

3 Reflective, triangular assessment framework

An important final step in any student-led activity is an assessment procedure that can reveal student perspectives on project progress and accomplishments. Establishing a Self-Peer-Teacher assessment framework permits greater transparency as it provides important insights into the overall project experience, while it also enhances assessment reliability through a triangular 'checks and balances' system. In the talk, examples of each assessment tool were introduced in addition to factors related to their design and implementation, such as the use of both task- and perception-based evaluation and project objective-based criteria.

Overall, these three project components effectively encourage self-directed, meaningful learning and help sustain motivated participation. Although implemented on a project-based course, many of the above suggestions can apply to a wide variety of group tasks, and can assist students in achieving a satisfying, personal understanding of new content areas.

E-mail: cynthiaquinn@yahoo.com

5.9 Using video recordings of TV commercials to teach grammar

Françoise Naski-Brown *Université de Picardie Jules Verne, Amiens, France*

I have found over the years that TV commercials can make excellent instructional materials for anyone wishing to teach grammar without resorting to tedious drilling. They obviously present a number of advantages:

- They are short, self-contained units; their length (roughly one minute, sometimes only a few seconds) is ideal for use in the classroom.
- If chosen well, they can be funny, original and striking, and help focus the learners' attention.
- They combine pictures and sound, and often a written message, which means that learners have to view, listen and read at the same time. The three elements can be exploited separately or jointly.
- Most British or American TV channels broadcast commercials. So it is fairly easy for teachers to get hold of them.
- TV commercials have become part of today's (teen) culture. And as we all know very well, using teaching materials which are familiar to, and popular with, the learners can only prove beneficial.

Of course, the grammar points you choose to introduce, or revise, with your students depend upon the type of TV commercial you use. As I cannot refer here to specific examples, I am just going to provide a few general guidelines which should be applicable to different types of commercials. Here are a few recurrent patterns, and suggestions for their exploitation:

1 **The *puzzling* commercial**: in some commercials, it is not quite clear until the very end what is being advertised. With these, it is easy to truncate the final message (usually text which appears on the screen at the last minute) and make the students practise modals: 'It *may well be* an advertisement for ...'; 'It *could be advertising* ...'

2 **The *disaster* commercial**: commercials very often show a character who is having problems. Play the commercial once, so that the students know what happens in it. Then you can either freeze the picture just *before* a mishap and ask them to tell you what is *about to* happen: 'She's *going to* drop her plate' or 'She's *about to* stain her T-shirt'. Or you might prefer to freeze the picture just *after* the mishap, and ask the students to describe what *has just happened.*

3 **The *comparison* commercial**: sometimes, in commercials, a comparison is made between two situations: one where the product advertised is used, and another where a 'conventional' product is used. With this type of commercial, it is easy to practise comparatives: 'Jane's sheets are *cleaner than* Mary's' or 'John's car is *more beautiful*

than Ken's.' Alternatively, you can revise markers of contrast: 'Mrs Smith uses X soap powder *whereas* Mrs MacDonald uses Y.' With more advanced students, it is also possible to drill conditional sentences: '*If* Jack *had used* the Z washing liquid, his dishes *would have been* cleaner.'

E-mail: fnaski@wanadoo.fr

5.10 Integrating online materials into the EFL classroom

Eva Daughn and Margaret Callow *Bell Language School, Saffron Walden, England*

Overview

The talk focussed on two lesson plans, using non-EFL websites and, in one instance, using both EFL and non-EFL websites to develop a series of lessons. Follow-up activities were included. The underlying rationale in choosing any website should be to look at ways of preparing generic materials for sites that are likely to be long-lasting, in order to save time and energy for everyone.

Teaching implications

Clear instructions, achievable within the lesson time constraints, should be stated at the beginning of the lesson.

- There is a great deal of information on the World Wide Web, with the added lure of hyperlinks to countless other sites. Instructions for navigation to the sites you want students to look at need to be very clear; otherwise students surf aimlessly and may produce nothing.
- Because the language on non-EFL web sites is not graded, some vocabulary preparation and information on how to navigate the site needs to be outlined in a guided worksheet. It is always wise to sensitise the students to the topic and state clear aims which strike a balance between the freedom to roam, e.g. find their own newspaper articles, and getting lost or overwhelmed by the sheer amount of language.
- At the end of the lesson, ask students to comment on the sites, layout and how easily navigable they were.

EXAMPLE LESSON 1
Saint Valentine's Day

Aims:

- Background on Saint Valentine's Day
- Vocabulary
- Reading
- Speaking

PART 1 (In the classroom)

http://www.pictureframes.co.uk/pages/saintvalentine.htm#traditions had information in small chunks which could easily be printed, cut up and stuck on a worksheet. This was taught as an information gap activity in which all the students had the same questions, but only half the information. They then exchanged information with a partner to answer all the questions.

PART 2 (In the computer room)
The Language Exerciser (Intermediate 1) in the Multimedia exercises on an EFL website, www.bellenglish.com, contains exercises on Festivals and Saint Valentine's Day.

1 Text-builder – students listen to a recording in pairs and reconstruct the text.
2 Multiple choice (Focus on Linkers) – students read the same passage in pairs with linking words omitted, but with three multiple choice options given.
3 Follow-up activities – A local survey; write a Valentine card; write a poem.

EXAMPLE LESSON 2
Using newspapers and non-EFL online newspaper web sites

1 Prior to going online, students spent one lesson looking at actual newspapers, using a worksheet.
2 The next lesson involved:
   - scanning for headlines
   - evaluating websites for layout, content, difficulty in navigating sites
   - reading for detail to find out about one article
   - summarising an article

Websites used in the preparation of materials
www.cnn.co.uk
www.bbc.co.uk/newsround
www.bbc.co.uk/news
www.mirror.co.uk
www.thetimes.co.uk
www.bellenglish.com

5.11 Creating an online learning environment for media English courses

Haruo Nishinoh *Doshisha University, Kyoto, Japan*

The advent of high-powered multi-media-handling computers has enabled teachers to produce digitised videos on CD-ROM. These videos, when combined with online materials, can create an inexpensive and effective learning environment for ESL-CALL classes. This is especially useful for media English courses where there is a need for timely authentic materials and individualised learning.

Both online and off-line resources are used. Video on demand, which requires a high-speed connection, is replaced by CD-ROMs, and other materials are provided through WWW home pages. Being built on readily available software and network facilities, this environment is easy to create and maintain.

The first step is to record TV news reports. An ordinary VCR can be used for this purpose. When reports are selected, they are digitised and saved on CD-ROM disks. One 640MB CD-ROM disk will hold more than 60 minutes of MPEG-1 video of reasonably high resolution.

The second step is to create study materials. These are Microsoft Word or HTML documents consisting of preview quizzes, in-class drills, and assignments. This process is greatly facilitated when transcripts are available. Most of the American news companies post their transcripts on the LEXIS-NEXIS full-text database (www.lexis.com), and some provide them fully (www.cnn.com) or in part (abcnews.go.com) on the Internet.

The third step is to create WWW pages, where these study materials are to be delivered. Any page-authoring tool and ftp software can be used. These pages can be hosted on a school server, or in one of those free (geocities.yahoo.com) or inexpensive (www.web.com) Web hosting services.

A class session starts with viewing class home pages for the day. Then the whole class study preview quizzes. After this, students are given CD-ROMs and individually start working on the video. (For copyright reasons, CD-ROMs should be used only in the classroom and should be retrieved after the session.) Study materials are carefully structured, so that, as students work on them, they come to grasp the main idea and then understand the details. Assignments consist of online search activities and short essay writing. Students are encouraged to learn how to gather pieces of relevant information, sort them out, and use them for their own creative writing process in their essays. They are also encouraged to access the full-text database individually to obtain their own copies of transcripts after the session. The teacher's role during the session is as facilitator of individual studies. S/he also gives comments to each student on their assignments for the past week.

In the fall of 2001, the course had 13 sessions in two classes of 25 students each. 10 digitised news reports were used. Pre- and post-tests show students' general improvement in listening, writing and vocabulary. Students found the digitised materials fun and easy to work with. Accessibility to transcripts and other online resources helped improve their writing and vocabulary. In addition to this, most of the students, through regular use of the Internet news sites, became highly aware of current and cross-cultural issues.

E-mail: hnishino@mail.doshisha.ac.jp

5.12 Learning language through science: An evaluation of the Science Across Europe project

Miyoko Kobayashi *University of Warwick*

This paper presented findings from an evaluation of the Science Across Europe (SAE) project. SAE is an international science education project initiated in the early 1990s with the aim of bringing a global dimension to science education. Its materials were developed to encourage students in secondary schools across Europe to work on everyday science topics such as 'food' and 'domestic waste' and to exchange ideas and findings with students in other countries. Of particular interest to language educators is the dual aim of SAE to promote the use of a foreign language, both in working on the science-oriented materials and in the exchange of information with schools in other countries, possibly through the use of information and communications technology. With the more recent shift in emphasis to the foreign language teaching dimension, greater involvement of foreign language teachers has been encouraged. The project itself is premised on a number of assumptions from a range of areas in applied linguistics such as bilingual education, content-based language teaching, collaborative teaching/learning, self-directed learning, and the use of information technology (see, for example, Brown & Brown 1998, Cummins & Swain 1986, Ellis & Sinclair 1989, Fried-Booth 1986, Johnson & Swain 1997, Liaw 1994, Nunan 1992, Thompson 1993, Warschauer 1997).

The University of Warwick undertook an evaluation of the SAE programme, from the language learning viewpoint, by means of a questionnaire survey administered to approximately 60 teachers and 600 learners in 13 countries. Areas of particular interest included: experience in SAE; gender differences; approaches to SAE; and comparison of the new users before and after using the SAE materials.

The findings suggested that the SAE project had had a positive impact on aspects of language learner motivation, with some evidence for enhanced foreign language learning achievement. In particular, exchange activities were perceived to be useful for promoting language learning. This corresponds to the accepted view that use of a foreign language for genuine communication enhances learning. However, in the new classes where teachers adopted a collaborative approach, this did not seem to be particularly successful either in enhancing learners' motivation or promoting their language learning. This finding seemed to echo Nunan (*Collaborative Language Learning and Teaching* CUP 1992), who sets out some of the conditions that must be fulfilled if educational innovations – such as collaboration – are going to work. When comparing boys and girls, there were some indications that girls benefited more than boys from using SAE, especially when SAE was used for science learning.

The paper also discussed questions relating to methodology in the evaluation of language-in-education projects. In a real educational context, it may be necessary to accept some limitations when conducting research – especially commissioned research – because of potential conflicts of interest between researchers and funding bodies or other stakeholders.

Despite the shortcomings in the research methodology, the findings had important implications for applied linguistics: foreign language teaching could be broadened and enriched by combining it with other subjects. SAE materials seem to provide good opportunities for diversifying foreign language classrooms, with clear benefits for learners.

E-mail: Miyoko.Kobayashi@warwick.ac.uk

5.13 Sensible uses of the senses in English Language Teaching

Palmer Acheson *Concordia University, Montreal, Canada*

The presenter asked each member of the audience to imagine that they were travelling through a country ruled by a cruel dictator. He continued, saying, 'His police arrest you for a crime you did not commit. You are condemned to lose one of your five senses. Write them down: Hearing, Sight, Smell, Taste, and Touch. Which one do you sacrifice? Write the number 1 beside the one you give up. Hurry! The alternative is death! You lose it. Later, the police chief returns and tells you that you have been condemned for another crime, and must lose a second sense. Choose one. Write the number 2 beside it. You have three left. Alas, the police chief returns, and again relays the absurd "judgement" of his political masters: you must sacrifice a third sense. Write number 3 beside it. You hope this is the end of it, but a second police chief comes to see you (his predecessor has been executed), and tells you that you are only allowed to keep one sense. Write the number 4 beside the one you give up. Now write a 5 beside the one you have left.'

A rough tally of the responses revealed that the majority of the audience first gave up the sense of smell, followed by taste, touch, and hearing (keeping the sense of sight to the last). However, many people did not follow this sequence, demonstrating that they valued their senses differently from the average responses. Over five years, while surveys of 204 teachers have revealed a consistent tendency to value the senses of hearing and sight more than others, there is considerable variation among subjects, particularly with regard to the relative importance of the senses of smell, taste and touch.

The moral of this exercise? In teaching, we must remember to cater to different students and their preferred different learning strategies! The language teaching methods that styled themselves 'audio-visual' were definitely exploiting the two most valued senses, but, as hearing- and/or sight-impaired people amply demonstrate, it is possible to become a highly developed human being while lacking one or even both of these senses.

During the remaining ten minutes of the presentation, we examined some lesson plans which exploited the three neglected senses of smell, taste, and touch. The plans are structured in such a way as to be executable with a wide range of students in terms of age and language ability. Blindfolding students heightens these three ways of perceiving the world. Realia (e.g. fruit, flowers, cologne/soap samples) is easily obtained for 'smelly' activities; a blind taste test (e.g. Coke vs. 7Up) is always enjoyable, especially when advocates of one or the other cannot tell the difference when blindfolded; feeling substances that are rough, smooth, hard, soft, heavy, cold, metallic, etc. increases one's vocabulary in a realistic and memorable way. Finally, surveys are a motivating and highly interactive activity requiring the asking and answering of questions about gustatory preferences.

E-mail: acheson@alcor.concordia.ca

5.14 A taste of literature

Lisa Nazarenko and Gillian Schwarz *University of Vienna, Austria*

Literature is an important element of language and culture. Yet, there is often not enough time on a course for students to read and work with an entire play or novel. One option is to use short stories for class discussion. However, since many students are not interested in reading, even in their own language, the common approach of 'read at home and discuss in class' often results in routinised lessons that engage few of the students.

In choosing texts to work with, we take into account the students' level and areas of interest. We prefer scenes or extracts that involve interaction between two people and in which that interaction tells its own story (i.e. is not dependent on knowing what came before). The scene should be rich in dialogue, and preferably have one or more filmed versions. Examples of texts that we have used with our upper-intermediate level university students are: the marriage proposal scene from *The Importance of Being Earnest*; the opening scene of *Death of a Salesman*; the balcony scene from *Romeo and Juliet*; Catherine's death scene from *Wuthering Heights*; and the choice we used for our IATEFL presentation, the marriage proposal scene between Elizabeth and Mr Darcy in *Pride and Prejudice*. We wanted participants to experience the activities as students might, and we therefore chose a scene that we use with advanced students.

Students read the scene at home, and in class review what they understand of the scene and the interaction between the two characters (e.g. how they each feel, how their feelings change, what they are doing during the scene, how they are speaking, etc). After preparatory work on differences in intonation, inflection and stress, students practise speaking the opening dialogue of the scene, in order to compare their versions of how these lines could be said. Another activity involves their rewriting these lines in contemporary English. This helps students get a better feel for what the characters are saying and what they really mean, as well as giving them practice in creating realistic dialogue in English. In the final activity, students form groups to discuss how they would stage this scene if they were filming it. They are encouraged to include as much detail as is suggested to them by the extract. Students are able to see that there are many possible interpretations of the text, and through this activity they develop more confidence in their view of the scene. In a follow-up lesson, students compare their versions with three filmed versions that we present in class. These versions display a great range of differences in all aspects of the scene. It is not only entertaining for the students to see the variations, but shows them again that many interpretations are possible.

These ideas can be used together or separately for a variety of novels and plays in all types of language classes.

E-mail: lisa.nazarenko@aon.at
schwarzg@gmx.net

5.15 Body and song

Torsten Sommer *Bildungszentrum der Stadt Nürnberg, Germany*

The intention of the workshop was to present and experiment with an unconventional, but not at all new, approach to the use of songs, characterised by the following main features:

- The learners are given no written presentation of the song texts.
- The learners hear the song performed by the teacher, but not from a recording.
- The performer 'acts out' the song, using the 'whole body', facial expression and gesticulation, encouraging the listener to imitate those when they repeat the lines.
- The learners try to recover the words from memory, helping each other, until they reconstruct the whole text.
- The learners do not have to do exercises on the language content of the songs.

The rationale for this approach is based on the following observations and assumptions:

- Singing a song from a printed text often leads learners to make mistakes in pronunciation, even if they are given a good model from the teacher's singing or from a recording, because learners often make assumptions about pronunciation from the written representation, e. g. sounding of 'silent' sounds, pronouncing weak forms strongly, not connecting words because they are separated by gaps, etc.
- Not being able to refer to the text sheet, learners have to concentrate much more intensively on listening and watching. By responding physically, learners are more open to the overall meaning, or story, of the text, even without understanding every single word, and have to be aware of the meaning in order to memorise it. Apparently, the 'acting out' is inseparable from the meaning and is easier to remember than words learnt merely by rote; and the gesticulation, when watched and repeated, triggers the words that belong to them.
- Provided that the teacher chooses songs suitable for this kind of approach, the learners are able to memorise lengthy texts within a short time. Rediscovering that they have this ability, which, with practice, can facilitate language learning enormously, strengthens the learners' confidence in their language learning abilities.
- People enjoy singing most when they sing merely for pleasure, not for the explicit purpose of learning language, and when singing is an interactive group experience. Given that an activity that emotionally engages and involves the learners will facilitate learning, it is not always necessary to complement a singing activity with exercises on the language content, because the learners will take away those bits of language which are relevant for them.

The main objective of the workshop was to try out the practical implementation of the above principles, i.e. to learn songs from listening, watching and repeating only, and to sing them together, in which most of the audience engaged with great enthusiasm, several participants contributing songs themselves. Some participants would have liked to discuss the principles underlying this approach, which is based primarily on anecdotal evidence and has to await scrutiny in the light of future results from SLA research, but regrettably this was outside the scope of this practice-orientated workshop.

E-mail: toson@t-online.de

5.16 Bringing the real world into the classroom

Sheila Thorn *The Listening Business, London, England*

I began my talk by outlining why I feel strongly that if we are to prepare our students adequately for the real world outside the classroom, the listening texts found in coursebooks need to be supplemented with recordings of radio programmes designed for native speakers.

Publishers understandably do not want their coursebooks to become dated. Nor do they want to risk causing offence. As a result, coursebooks are situated in an alternative, sterile world where nothing awful ever happens – no one is made redundant, no one becomes seriously ill, no one is the victim of crime, no one becomes addicted to drugs, and so on. Yet these real world issues are too important to be ignored and should, I feel, be tackled in the safe environment of the classroom. Other reasons for using off-air recordings include the fact that the listening texts in coursebooks are generally graded in terms of lexis and structures, scripted to some extent and spoken at a much slower speed than in the real world, generally in neutral accents. They do not therefore reflect the varieties of English the students are likely to encounter outside the classroom.

By exposing students to off-air recordings we can help them overcome the three main problems they have with listening, which are:

- distinguishing individual words in a stream of speech
- lack of familiarity with much of the lexis they hear
- difficulty in understanding non-standard accents.

In my talk I outlined the types of programmes which can be used successfully in the classroom, including news, reports, interviews, phone-ins and arts programmes. I then talked about how recent developments have made it possible to download radio programmes from the Internet days, or even months, after transmission.

There are some excellent programmes available on the BBC Radio 4 website (www.bbc.co.uk/radio4). These include *From Our Own Correspondent*, which features reports from BBC correspondents all over the world. Transcripts of the programmes are available on the programme's home page.

Crossing Continents looks at topical issues in a different country each week and often features interviews with non-native speakers. It also has an archive of programmes going back to 1998.

Woman's Hour also provides excellent listening practice. The home page contains an index of topics covered in each programme during the week and the teacher can go back week by week over a period of several months to select suitable topics. Other suitable programmes are *Home Truths* (featuring listeners' anecdotes), *Leading Edge* (scientific breakthroughs), *Home Planet* (environmental issues) and *You and Yours* (consumer issues).

In the next part of my talk, I gave general tips for writing exercises focused on language areas as well as traditional listening comprehension. I concluded my talk by giving advice on how to use off-air recordings in the classroom: the need for praise and encouragement, particularly in the early stages, ways of making students see listening practice as a challenge rather than a test and ideas for fully exploiting lexis.

I would be happy to send a summary of my talk by e-mail if requested.

E-mail: sthorn@clara.net

5.17 Cultures alive! Multicultural education using folk tales and folk dances

Michele Milner *International Christian University, Japan*

The following activities were designed to introduce multicultural concepts to Japanese elementary school students in a holistic learning environment that encouraged whole-body thinking and self-expression. Involving both the cognitive and kinaesthetic senses can heighten conceptual awareness, increase 'memorability' and stimulate creative problem-solving. Children are experiential learners and movement is one of the most important ways in which they learn. Using movement-based activities to introduce English allows them physically to experience the concepts and emotions associated with language study. Words and concepts take on deeper emotional resonance and become more integrated into their thought-world.

Folk tales model authentic language and stimulate listening because of an interest in the story. Less emphasis is placed on grammar in favour of a broader understanding of the story elements and sequence. Students learn to become less fearful of not understanding every word, and adopt a more relaxed and confident feeling towards the study of English. Active listening techniques focus on key elements and heighten participation in storytelling. Various methods of re-telling serve as scaffolding to foster emerging speech production. Picture cards, choral reading and dramatisation are effective tools to develop speech, without appealing to explicit knowledge of grammar.

Folk dancing is done by ordinary people, so requires no special training. Every culture uses dance to express human emotions, transcending language as a form of expression. The dances demonstrate a sense of community, requiring the participants to work together co-operatively. Teaching them using English recycles action verbs in context. Students translate their understanding directly into their own bodies; an empowering consolidation of mind–body thinking.

Starting with a folk story from Mali, the presenter demonstrated how to use props effectively in storytelling, and a co-operative re-telling technique with picture cards. This was followed by an African drumming warm-up to increase awareness of rhythm, and a chanting activity based on the story. Lastly, the isolated body movements of African dance were explored, and participants were given a chance to express their interpretation of the chant using these movements. The presenter showed a folktale from Denmark called *The Fat Cat* and demonstrated *The 7 Jumps Dance*. The dance adds simple steps to a basic pattern. Likewise, the story is about a cat that eats a succession of items. These were combined to produce a circle dance/chant. Lastly, students drew an abstract representation of a story as a 'path', and then tried to use movement to represent their drawing.

Some of the participants wondered if the level of difficulty of the language was a problem. However, the presentation of material in a variety of modes (visual, verbal, movement) enables most children to comprehend the stories and then express their understanding in a variety of ways. When teaching the cultural aspects of these stories and dances, flexibility is the key. They can be used as cultural artefacts, TPR tools or creative stimuli for movement, writing and speaking. These activities are meant to give students a variety of modes to both access and express their understanding of culturally relevant material.

E-mail: milnermw@yahoo.com

5.18 'It's like what?' Fact and fiction in teaching language and culture

Joanne Collie *University of Warwick, England* and **Antoinette Moses** *Freelance, England*

Joanne Collie began by making some remarks about the necessary interrelations between teaching language and culture. The focus was on three questions: Firstly 'Why is the cultural dimension essential?' Reasons discussed included:

- Understanding is rooted in an L1 context to begin with, shaped by prior expectations.
- Language is a social practice, with meaning negotiated within specific cultural situations.
- Cultural awareness is increasingly needed for effective communication and for coping with difference in an ever more globalised world.

The second question: 'Why a comparative approach?' reviewed the rationale for using comparative perspectives, to promote personal involvement, bring out and highlight the 'invisible' assumptions that are part of our own culture, and help to restore parity to different cultures, thus avoiding asymmetries of power.

Thirdly 'Why is fiction important?' demonstrated that 'facts' in a fictionalised context could make them more memorable, provide greater motivation by appealing to the students' own lives, and enable them to move beyond the stereotypes so often built into teaching patterns. Fiction could, in addition, provide valuable examples of English in actual use, and prompt students to use their new language in creative and interactive ways.

Finally, some examples from *What's It Like?* (Joanne Collie & Alex Martin CUP 2000) were used to show how the 'actual' language used by teenagers (in this case recordings of interviews with students discussing their relationship with their parents) matched and extended that of teenagers in the many excellent works of fiction currently available.

In the second half of the talk, Antoinette Moses explored how culture and language are interconnected in fiction. As a writer of fiction, she said, language was what shaped her writing – it was the paint, the clay, the notes of the music. It was through language that she found the voice – the voice that created character that drove the plot. When you write dialogue in English, every word, every inflection, reveals character, class and background. She then analysed three short extracts from her short-story collection, *Frozen Pizza and other slices of life* (CUP 2002) to demonstrate the way in which colloquial language can reveal intra-cultural differences. She picked out several examples from these stories in which the word 'like' was used with different meanings, and showed how graded fiction could provide examples of language in use.

These short stories also offered a variety of ways to explore British culture. Each one of them had been written not simply as a story, but to link with the unit themes in *What's It Like?* She read several extracts dealing with contemporary issues such as gangs, bullying, football hooliganism, truancy, broken homes, child poverty and the power of the media. The cultural references, she noted, were part of each story, but would also stimulate class discussions.

Through such fiction, she argued, students could find slices of the real world, of life in Britain today ... with multiculturalism, British weather, hobbies, teenage angst, poverty, injustice and, of course, frozen pizza.

E-mail: jmacollie@aol.com
amoses@btinternet.com

5.19 Exposing hidden cultures in teaching and learning: International cases

Dr Shosh Leshem *Academic College of Education Oranim, Israel and*
Dr Vernon Trafford *Anglia Polytechnic University, England*

This paper illustrated how cultural background directly affected patterns of teachers' oral feedback and the resulting classroom interaction by teachers and learners.

The three-year research study investigated foreign language teaching, and specifically English taught in Israel, as a particularly complex field of study. These types of teaching involved encounters between the classroom cultural setting and the culture underlying the target language.

The teacher's oral feedback was chosen owing to its critical role in classroom interaction, particularly in foreign language teaching, since the acquisition of the target language is largely dependent on meaningful communication. The interactional web of relationships between culture–language dependence, cultural diversity due to the dynamic nature of culture, and the role of feedback in the learning process of a foreign language, represented the conceptual framework for this research.

The paper presented data collected through an ethnographic approach to participant observation, in three discretely different cultural settings of Israeli Junior High School EFL classrooms: Jewish secular, Jewish ultra-Orthodox and Arab. This data was supplemented by evidence from professional diaries and interviews with school principals, teachers and learners. Action research-based cameo case studies from India, Singapore and Sri Lanka added further dimensions on the teaching and learning processes.

The analysis revealed distinctive micro-cultures, which reflected elements of each specific macro-culture. Patterns of oral feedback and the resultant interactional modes typifying each cultural context were illustrated.

Conclusions showed how these elements affected the language teaching and learning process, and its implications for the distance between the cultural background of teachers and students and the culture of the target language. Highlighting the complexity of classrooms in their socio-cultural contexts showed that teaching English as a foreign language is an encounter of cultures and not merely a linguistic experience. Evidence showed that the predominant cultural backgrounds of teachers and their students determine the nature of initial TEFL feedback provided in classrooms. Thus, the practical implications of this research related directly to teaching and learning in general and the field of TEFL in particular.

Conclusions were that teacher educators who prepare novice teachers from different cultural backgrounds to teach in their own social frameworks, should assist them to recognise their respective social frameworks and then to cope with cultural gaps. Teachers of English in Israeli schools should be educated to exploit the possibilities inherent in the subject, to promote tolerance and seek mutual understanding. Teachers of English as a foreign language need to recognise and account for cultural impact on their respective curriculum content, teaching strategies, experiential learning and assessment processes.

This conceptualisation could assist teachers and researchers to connect the micro- and macro-cultural spheres of their work. The practical and positive consequences for teachers and teacher trainers of appreciating the educational significance of ever-present socio-cultural dimensions in their classrooms were highlighted. Thus, the presentation assisted professional educators to reflect upon their respective teaching styles and the resultant learning consequences when teaching English as a foreign language.

E-mail: Shosh-l@internet-zahav
v.n.trafford@apu.ac.uk

6 DEBATES

6.1 Colloquium: Writing and publishing: Can creativity and profit live together?

Chairs: Jill Florent *Freelance, England,* **Gillian Porter Ladousse** *Freelance, France,* **Melanie Williams** *Freelance, France*
Panel: Martin Bates *Freelance, England,* **Susan Holden** *Publisher, Scotland,* **Péter Medgyes** *Eötvös Loránd University, Budapest, Hungary,* **Mario Rinvolucri** *Pilgrims, England*

Overview

Jill Florent *Freelance, England*

This was a colloquium for those interested in ELT publishing: writers, publishers, distributors and teachers aired the problems of incorporating creative ideas in ELT publishing which is profitable and also ethical.

The session was organised in four sessions:

Inform
What are the main problems and issues in ELT publishing today?

Connect
How can we make fruitful connections between new and experienced writers and publishers, small and large, to their mutual benefit?

Protect
How can writers protect themselves against unethical practices?
How can we protect creativity and originality in writing in a context of global 'blanding down'? How can we protect the rights of teachers to have access to materials which are context-sensitive?

Project
How can we set up mechanisms (networking, future events, etc.) to keep these issues alive and to create a group consciousness of them?

Participants were welcomed (on video) by Alan Maley. The members of the panel each made an opening statement. Martin Bates talked about his experiences as a successful coursebook author and self-published poet. Susan Holden spoke about being a publisher for a large company, a small company and about being a writer. With a foot in each camp, she was able to see both sides of the argument and appreciate the frustrations of authors as well as the needs of publishers. Péter Medgyes was asked to describe the differences between UK and non-UK publishers as he has written for both. He warned non-native speakers not to expect UK publishers to make allowances, and his list of *do*s and *don't*s for authors included 'Don't be born a non-native speaker'. Mario Rinvolucri publishes a webzine, and extolled the virtues of this type of publishing – there is, for example, no restriction on extent, an article can be as long as the author likes, because there is no 'page' to fit the copy into.

After these opening remarks, the debate was opened to the floor. There were publishers, published authors and would-be authors among the participants. Mario was challenged on two fronts: firstly, in talking about publishers' output, he had said that he 'abhorred coursebook publishing', and was asked to say why. I remain baffled by Mario's response 'This is a pen.' And as no one else took this further, I think most of the audience were, too. I can only say, that if that's what you're reduced to when using what's around you in the classroom, try opening a coursebook! Secondly, Adrian Tennant pointed out that most of the world has no access to computers, so web publishing is not democratic and inclusive, but restricted to the privileged.

Many people in the audience had come wanting to know how to get published. Their ideas had been rejected on the grounds that they 'didn't fit the publishing plan' or 'didn't have a wide enough appeal'. Susan explained that publishers have plans that stretch forward for three or five years, and most material is commissioned, leaving very little room for unsolicited manuscripts, and that sending a finished script was almost bound to end in rejection. Others said that they had posted lesson ideas on the web, but that although the free 'tasters' were eagerly downloaded, no one was prepared to pay for more material. They felt that they had indeed invented a better mousetrap, and could not understand why the world was not beating a path to their door. Mario replied that you have to be ready to give away an enormous amount of material to establish the quality and desirability of your ideas before you could hope to sell a little. Web publishing is not a way to get rich quick.

Some good advice for would-be authors came from a publisher in the audience: study publishers' catalogues, get the names of the commissioning editors in the most likely company, offer to do reader's reports and write workbook materials, refuse to take no for an answer and 'give them no peace'. Dave Allan invited people to join MATSDA (the Materials Development Association).

Another very good piece of advice is to join the Society of Authors, who can help writers with the business side of relationships with publishers. Members of the Society led a discussion of the new Educational Writing and Publishing Guidelines, which the Society has drawn up to replace the Publishers Association Code of Practice. The aim of the Guidelines is to establish good working relations between publishers and authors from the outset of a project. They cover the writing and publishing process from the time a proposal is submitted to the promotion of the published work. Members of the audience who were writers contributed examples from their own experience, which illustrated that such a document would be valuable, especially to new authors. Publishers, who might have been apprehensive about the content of the Guidelines, seemed to acknowledge their value. It is therefore hoped that when the Guidelines have been given final approval, authors will receive a copy from their publishers when they are invited to submit a proposal.

A few observations on creativity and profit

Martin Bates *Freelance, England*

'Good books don't sell.' Although this is an oversimplification, there's no denying the difficulty good authors find in maintaining quality (imaginative content, educational value, appropriateness and range, creativity) under the pressures on time, cost, format, etc. imposed by the market. It is also often the case that publishing managers with little knowledge of or interest in the creative process – from writing to learning – find bad authors much more amenable than good authors. The pressures working against creativity and genuine innovation have intensified, with increasing competition and dwindling numbers of major publishers. Books are generally seen as products and yet:

- They arise out of processes – teaching/writing/design/editing/revising/illustrating and – underlying all this – learning.
- They embody potential for process – teaching, learning, performing, developing competence.
- These processes have inevitably to be frozen by publishing.

I think a good book balances process and product, and makes it possible to turn product back into process. The dominant process among publishers is selling, and this can wreck the balance if it becomes all-important, which seems to happen in big companies driven primarily by competition with rivals. The following are trends I have observed, often painfully; there are, of course, exceptions.

- Selling is short-lived and makes for short shelf-life. This works against the long-term development, through trial and error, necessary to produce books combining quality with appropriateness. Management seems also to suffer from this short-termism, as those in charge of projects get shunted on, up or out, and there is a lack of continuity.
- Selling may become obsessed with covers and titles rather than content.
- It tends to become too self-absorbed, have its own ideas of what the market needs and believe its own propaganda.
- It is driven by the need to counter competition and this tends to blur long-term vision.
- It doesn't know much about teaching or writing, and perhaps doesn't want to know, because that would make life too complicated.
- It may prefer to use people whose main concern is selling to do everything, including the writing; some at least of the more mindless books are actually written by people who emerge out of the book-production industry and have little or no experience of teaching.
- It can only see books as finished products and can't stand the mess of the writing process with its need to experiment and rewrite.

On the same level of generality, I will suggest conditions encouraging good work, based again on my own experience as, on the one hand, part of a team writing an ESP series at the chalk-face (*Nucleus*) and, on the other, an author writing at publishers' behest courses (*NILE, Welcome to English*) for Middle Eastern schools, where there was a gulf between what I knew of local conditions and what was known by UK-based management:

- Writers and other 'makers' often work in isolation, but there is a need for a sense of community. In some ways, the electronic revolution has made this more possible, but a more dubious effect has been the reduction of face-to-face meetings, which encourage friendly relations and minimise misunderstanding.
- Ideas may spring from ... who knows where? – but are best fertilised in relationships with others – with other teachers, writers, experts, etc. There is a need to bounce ideas off one another. Conditions for writing *Nucleus* were generally good, as we worked closely with colleagues, could try out ideas and get instant feedback from the students, who enjoyed the creative side of the process. It was much more difficult to build creative relationships into the process of writing *NILE* and *Welcome*, but some sense of community was achieved through visits to schools and contacts with local people of all kinds. In the UK I felt I was writing in a vacuum. Feedback is essential.
- Management should be in the hands of people who like and are curious about process and content – is this possible these days? – people who will actually read the book!
- Management should make communication and sharing of knowledge paramount and try to preserve elementary politeness (e.g. answer letters and emails, send copies of books to all who helped make them).
- Timing should be realistic and allow for experimentation and rewriting.
- There should be a genuine need and opportunity for innovation arising out of the teaching situation.
- Materials should arise from real experience and there should be opportunities to learn from experience during the process. In fact, this will include a whole range of different experiences, but the prevailing one should be teaching and learning.
- The practical approach should be leavened by theory, but only lightly. Use metalanguage sparingly, except to impress bureaucrats perhaps!
- The experience should be enjoyable for all.

A foot in each camp

Susan Holden *Publisher, Scotland*

I began by asking who in the audience considered themselves a publisher, who considered themselves an author – and who considered themselves both. A sizeable number of people fell into the third category, and I said this was a good illustration of the impossibility of drawing hard and fast lines ('There is no longer any "sheep and goats" or "black and white" ').

That said, I felt there was still a huge amount of non-comprehension of the priorities and pressures – and even the creative and productive procedures gone through – at the opposite ends of this spectrum. There was a tendency among writers to talk about 'the publisher' as if this were one person – ignoring the fact that a publishing company was made up of a huge number of people with interlocking but different roles (accountants, lawyers, sales and production people as well as the more obvious 'tip of the iceberg' editors and promotion people).

I also pointed out that, with the emergence of huge publishing companies, company priorities and policies were often dictated elsewhere – outside the control of editors.

Publishing is a business, and both large and small companies have to go through the same kind of procedures and need projects to be profitable in the same way. What is different is the amount of overhead a big company has to recoup, and the actual amount of profit needed. The costs of producing books are much the same, as are marketing costs.

The rise of bigger companies, with long-term policies and financial forecasting, meant that it was harder for an author to get a 'one off' title accepted – since most titles were commissioned to fill a particular place in a particular market sector. However, there were two positive results of this:

- more smaller, specialist companies who could afford to do speculative publishing within their given field of expertise – and could do so very well;
- the need in bigger companies for people to work on parts of large projects: writing tests, workbooks and so on, which was an ideal way of picking up professional experience and making useful contacts.

Looking at the author's problems, I felt that many people in publishing companies were so bound by schedules, sales forecasts and costs that they sometimes forgot how important it was to understand the author's need for communication and discussion – and time to think, however tight the schedule.

Finally, I felt that some tensions were inevitable in such a complex activity, involving so many people and functions, as ELT writing and publishing. A comparison was made with the teacher–student relationship: both are part of the whole, both need each other, but both may have different priorities in their way of reaching an identical goal. Two-way communication about processes and pressures, and the reasons for decisions, was the best way of making sure that the individuals were aware that they inhabited the same world.

The non-UK/non-native constituency

Péter Medgyes *Eötvös Loránd University, Budapest, Hungary*

Identity crisis: Who am I? Can a person be identified by who they are NOT, instead of who they are? In any case, what constituencies/categories of authors can be set up?

Pure groups

1 'The islander' – natives living/publishing in the UK
2 'The expat' – natives living/publishing outside the UK
3 'The mainlander' – non-natives living/publishing outside the UK
4 'The defector' – non-natives living/publishing in the UK

Mixed groups

5 'The conquistador' – natives living in the UK, but publishing outside the UK
6 'The escapist' – natives living outside the UK, but publishing in the UK

7 'The homesick' – non-natives living in the UK, but publishing outside the UK
8 'The schizophrenic' – non-natives living outside the UK, but publishing in the UK

My writing career:

- I have lived all my life in Hungary and used to write books published locally for a Hungarian audience.
- In 1989 the Hungarian market was flooded by UK-published books.
- Hungarian coursebooks disappeared (UK-published books were glossy and more authentic, and Hungarian publishers were capital-poor).
- Certain gap-fillers have survived (e.g. test-books for special Hungarian examinations, bilingual dictionaries, two-language texts).

I was at a crossroads: should I stop writing? write gap-fillers? try my luck with UK publishers? I chose the last option.

What's it like to be schizophrenic?

Cons

- writing in a language which is not your own (unnatural + time-consuming)
- difficult to find materials
- hard to find your way into publishing (lack of connections)
- handicapped in terms of understanding rules of publishing (e.g. UK contracts and tax regulations)

Pros

- proving that English language/ELT has gone international
- outsider's fresh perspective
- challenge

Don'ts

- Don't be born a non-native author!
- Don't get (too) worried about your English Language handicap!
- Don't expect special treatment!
- Don't attach too much hope to becoming a mainstream author!

Dos

- Do take advantage of your 'foreign' perspective! (e.g. *Laughing Matters*)
- Do look for gaps in the market which only a non-native can discover! (e.g. *The Non-Native Teacher, Changing Perspectives in Teacher Education*)
- Do accept criticism with an open heart!
- Do publish at home, too.

Resource books on the Web

Mario Rinvolucri *Pilgrims, England*

My main contribution was to suggest that the future of teachers' resource books, which have carried so much of the innovative thinking in EFL over the past 30 years, probably lies in Web publication.

With the concentration of all UK EFL publishing in the hands of half a dozen major houses, less and less attention will be paid to these 'small books', which are seen by the big boys as a sad distraction from selling 'big books' like dictionaries and coursebooks.

The advantages of Web publication are as follows:

- Initial capital outlay required is small.
- Books full of exercises are a better bet on the Web than books full of continuous prose.
- The cost of putting the books up on the Web is tiny compared to printing and distributing traditional books, so teachers' resource books on the Web can be extremely cheap.
- On the Web, teachers' resource books will reach every corner of the globe, which is sadly not the case with printed teachers' resource books at £13 per copy.
- The production process will be down to under a month, compared to well over a year for most printed teachers' resource books.

The disadvantages of Web publication are these:

- It is hard to persuade EFL colleagues to pay for things on the Web.
- If you offer EFL ideas free on the Web, you may get 20,000 subscribers to your site. If you ask for modest payment, takers from among the 20,000 may be as few as 100–200.
- Many people feel that Web payments are not secure and there are reasons to think they are right.
- Many people, even young folk, are still wedded to the concept of the book as an object of huge cultural and personal worth.

6.2 The Graded Readers Debate

Chair: Catherine Walter *University of Reading, England*
Panel: Sarah Axten *Macmillan Education, England*, **Jennifer Bassett** *Freelance/OUP, England*, **Andy Hopkins** *Freelance/Pearson Education, England*, **Philip Prowse** *Freelance/CUP, England*

The editors of the four main UK series of graded readers joined forces to debate current issues in extensive reading. Catherine Walter, an authority on reading, was a fair and vigorous chair, and co-ordinated and paced the debate very effectively. The discussion considered viewpoints and issues raised in advance over the web by teachers worldwide, as well as by the audience on the day. Issues raised included authentic vs simplified materials, original stories versus simplifications, cultural taboos, use of readers and activities, the role of word lists, non-fiction and 'modern' stories, the use of recordings and the 'recalcitrant' reader. Each panellist began by answering the question: What makes a good graded reader?

Sarah Axten *Macmillan Education, England*

What makes a good graded reader? A 'good' graded reader has to inspire today's student and, hopefully, stand the test of time on the shelf. It doesn't matter how carefully prepared a story is in linguistic terms, if it doesn't fire the imagination and challenge the student with new, apposite language that they have the opportunity to absorb through repetition and recycling, they will lose interest. Students using an English reader should be able to engage with their book and expect an enjoyable experience. Reading should be an eagerly anticipated pleasure, not a demotivating and daunting task. If used extensively, the books can help create and nurture a reading habit and contribute to the development of writing and listening skills.

Taking it as a given that in creating a reading series, a sound structural grading system is in place, I believe that it is essential to reinforce the learning process for the student by providing as much support as possible. Notes on the background and context of the story as well as contextualised glossaries, attractive, descriptive and integrated artwork, and optional comprehension work are included in the Macmillan Guided Readers Series. We recognise the fact that a barrier to a student's successful acquisition of language lies not only in the language load they are expected to accept, but also the attendant information load. We have a global market – with end-users from greatly differing cultures, of all ages, abilities and requirements. They may be motivated or unmotivated. They may be in a classroom situation or working alone. And these assumptions drive our choice of material for the list.

Anticipating that this wide spectrum of learners has an equally varied range of tastes and interests, we provide original stories (fiction and non-fiction) covering a broad range of ideas and issues, as well as retold and simplified editions of modern and classic writing. While in recent years the selection of graded readers has been more greatly influenced by students' preferences for more fashionable and ephemeral subjects, in some quarters there is still the feeling that English is best represented by recognised works of literature. But whether it is original writing or specially retold versions of traditional or contemporary fiction, we look for a genre, title, subject or author's work that is a good example of its type – and which also appeals to the target audience. Strong themes and topics form the essential framework on which a good story is founded. But whether new areas are explored or well-trodden paths are revisited, we consider the cultural, political or religious sensitivity of the material in order not to unnecessarily offend. The age and gender of the protagonists are important to the learner – strongly drawn characters and the situations that they are placed in can contribute significantly to the success of a title.

The narrative flow and dialogue should be pertinent and as natural as possible and for this reason, we do not limit our writers to prescribed wordlists. If particular vocabulary is necessary to the progression and context of the story, they are encouraged to contextualise and repeat it as much possible. Many of our titles are available on audio and because the text is the audio script, we recognise the significance of the rhythm and flow of a story.

Writers are urged to pay attention to patterns of drama and tension within a plot that has a strong linear flow, so that the student wants to turn the pages. They are advised not only to control the language, but also carefully consider the information load (cultural and historical references, background and technical information, number of characters and subplots) and anticipate that not all their readership may be familiar with the context and setting.

To consolidate the pleasurable experience for the reader, we aim for the highest visual and production standards. Eye-catching covers and attractive artwork promote a 'read me' impression. The books should look and feel like real paperbacks and avoid overstating their educational agenda. A good graded reader should make no concessions on its production values.

Reflections on the debate

It was interesting to have confirmed how closely parallel the aims and intentions of our different series seem to run. The presentations echoed our firm belief that graded readers are invaluable tools in the language classroom and that they also provide invaluable support to coursebooks. Where we sometimes differed was in the way presentation in our readers is linked to their function. There is always the pressure from teachers to provide ever more intensive work for our extensive graded readers. But even if our individual lists may include, to a greater or lesser degree, teaching aids such as background notes, word definitions, artwork, activity/supplementary materials etc., we are all aiming for the same goal. That is to produce readers that we are proud to have published and that students and teachers find genuinely useful and appealing.

Jennifer Bassett *Freelance/OUP England*

What makes a good graded reader? My answer is very simple: a good story. Of course, there are other important elements in a good graded reader: an appropriate language code for the target level; attractive and clear presentation; and good support material. But if we compare a graded reader to a horse and cart, we might say that the story is the horse, and all these other elements are the cart. And, as everybody knows, if you put the cart before the horse, you don't go anywhere. So the horse – the story – must come first.

If a writer sets out to assemble appropriate linguistic data for pedagogic purposes, then almost certainly the resulting book will not be 'a good story'. The *underlying* pedagogical aim is to tell a story so fascinating, so unputdownable, that it draws readers into its fictional universe and holds them there until the end. It's no good having impeccably controlled lexis and structure if the story doesn't hold the reader's attention beyond the first page.

But what do we mean by 'a good story'? We should identify two components here: first, the story content (sometimes called the *fabula*), which is the series of events that take place in the fictional world. The second is the story-telling, by which I mean the plot, the organization, the artifices used in shaping these events into a narrative.

The story content is often less important than the shape it is given in the telling, and a question often asked is whether it is better to have an original story or an adaptation. The answer is that it is completely immaterial where the story content comes from –

whether from the writer's imagination, or from a previous writer's imagination, and is thus a retelling of an existing work of fiction. What matters is the story-telling; the key factor defining a good graded reader is the craftsmanship of the writing. Here is the novelist Philip Pullman on story-telling:

> It's craftsmanship. Your aim must be to tell a story as well as you can. You turn the raw materials, and all those loose bits of imagination and experience and memory, into something that stands up like a table with four legs and that doesn't fall over when you put your elbows on it.

Good craftsmanship is even more important when writing in a reduced language code. Weak plots, inadequate motivation, shaky narrative frameworks can sometimes hide behind the fig leaf of elaborate and convoluted language, but not in a graded reader – where of course we cannot have elaborate and convoluted language. The language in a graded reader has to be, of necessity, clean, spare, and minimalist – and every hole in a plot will be glaringly obvious.

Are there special rules for story-telling craftsmanship in graded readers? There are many, but two of the most important are these:

1 Avoid a simplistic approach to narrative structure, because a narrative that employs no artifices will rarely have the 'page-turning' factor.
2 Remember the reader, because if there is one characteristic that the community of L2 readers shares above all others, it is that they are very easily discouraged.

A well-told story, whether in a graded reader or anywhere else, will, as the novelist John Updike put it:

> ... instantly set in motion a certain forward tilt of suspense or curiosity.
>
> It will do this, preferably, by the end of the first page. And it will maintain this momentum throughout the narrative, keeping the pace moving, never losing the reader, setting up expectations, and satisfying them. Or, in the words of the Russian writer Anton Chekhov:
>
> If in the first chapter you say that a gun hung on the wall, in the second or third chapter it must without fail be discharged.

Reflections on the debate

Contributions to the debate, both those from the floor and those gathered previously from the Web, raised many of the questions often discussed in extensive reading. Is it better to read authentic materials rather than graded readers? What are the merits of original stories versus adaptations? What about cultural accessibility? And vocabulary acquisition? What is the role of wordlists? How should graded readers be used in a language course?

Panellists had no hesitation in putting the claims of comprehensibility higher than those of authenticity, and offered differing, though rarely opposing, views on other questions. The suggestion that adaptations were in principle inferior to original stories was firmly rebutted; always providing, of course, that the adapting or retelling (simplification is an inappropriate word for the process, in my view) is done with storytelling craftsmanship of a professional standard. As to how graded readers should be used, there were no definitive answers. Everybody has preferences, but at the same time we recognise that every learning context is different, and perhaps the most significant point to emerge from the discussions was the importance of choice – offering choice of genre, style, and cultural settings in stories; allowing choice of the most appropriate or effective way to use graded readers.

In sum, the world of graded readers is a broad church, and the panellists offered views ranging from the pragmatic and down-to-earth, to the aspirational and idealistic. We all accept that learners sometimes, perhaps often, have to be coaxed and cajoled and inveigled into extensive reading, by means of related activities and visual and auditory stimuli, but that does not mean that there is no room for idealistic goals as well. We must surely always live in hope that students will overcome the motivational barriers and learn to enjoy reading for the pleasure it brings as well as the improvement to their language skills. That is certainly the hope that underlies all my endeavours to make good graded readers, and in my mind's eye as I work, there is always an image of a student curled up in a corner with a book, utterly absorbed in a fictional universe.

Andy Hopkins *Freelance/Pearson Education, England*

As series editors, we aim to:

- provide books that learners want to read, presented in a manner that encourages them to do so – and that teachers feel are useful to the learning process;
- provide as much information as possible about the series – in particular about the level system;
- implement the level system in a manner that is consistent and open to scrutiny;
- provide as much optional support as possible for the reader – recognising that the books are for use in a learning context.

What makes a good reader?

- **Choice** – Essential to a good readers series. Teachers have their own reading preferences, but students don't necessarily share our tastes. Penguin Readers provide something for everyone – over 400 contemporary, classic and original fiction as well as non-fiction titles, catering for different ages, interests and levels of reading ability, in British and US English.
- **Careful selection of an original title** – For general appeal, it should be a good read, contain high-quality writing and be a well-known title and/or written by a well-known author. It may also have become a famous film. Features that affect a book's suitability for adaptation at a particular level include: complexity of plot, number of characters, proportion of dialogue to description, cultural accessibility and acceptability for use in educational contexts.
- **Acknowledging the strengths of the original work** – This is particularly important as many of our books are adaptations of the work of living authors. Our success in doing this is best assessed by the authors themselves, and we have had very supportive feedback from writers and copyright owners such as Kazuo Ishiguro, James Ellroy and Rowan Atkinson.

- **The quality of the story** – Of central importance. In a work of specially-written original fiction, the most important element is a well-chosen author – chosen for their credentials as a fiction writer, not on the basis of ELT experience, although the two may coincide. Many of the originals on our list are by established Puffin authors.
- **A powerful cover** – Persuades learners to select an unfamiliar title. A good start will grab readers' attention and encourage them to read on.
- **Clear language guidelines** – Hunch and experience are not, in our opinion, an appropriate basis for the language in a readers series. Whose hunches? Whose experience? How do you maintain a notion of level?
- **Maximum support for learners and teachers** – See our website for paper-based and online support materials.

Responses to some questions raised

Shouldn't learners be reading authentic texts?

The key to encouraging reading is to prepare learners for success by providing texts that interest, motivate and can be read without constant reference to a dictionary. It is not easy finding long authentic texts that grab students' attention, maintain interest and are of about the right level.

What is the role of wordlists?

There are (at least) four important questions to ask: a) Are titles written to wordlists? b) Were the lists compiled on sound principles? c) Are they open to scrutiny? d) Are they applied systematically?

Series editors must answer these questions clearly and positively; wordlists and structure lists are one of the key ways in which level is specified. We took as our starting point the *Longman Defining Vocabulary*, used to define all words in Longman learners' dictionaries. These in turn are based on data from the British National Corpus. Additional input came directly from the BNC, Council of Europe lists and an analysis of coursebooks. But in any particular book, twenty additional words (thirty at higher levels) are allowed, to recognise that key words in a story may not have high general frequency. These words are highlighted in activities at the back of the book.

If wordlists are too flexible, then the 'level' of the text can only be based on the writer's hunches and experience – which may not be shared with other writers. Intuitive writers may well write *below* the level, instead of pushing at the upper margins of a learner's likely reading ability.

Should we take account of the cultural taboos of various cultures?

In an ideal world, no. – A story is infused with the author's own cultural knowledge and assumptions, so the cultural backdrop is a key feature. But one must consider learners' educational contexts and cultural environments – and, of course, their age. These will affect the choice of a book for adaptation and the explicitness with which certain elements of a story are treated. Teachers and education authorities are far more likely to accept lack of censorship in higher-level titles, generally read by older learners – and, interestingly, in classics rather than in contemporary and original works.

We should select books carefully, taking advice on cultural taboos from the publisher's global representatives, and provide relevant information about a book's content. We assume, of course, that teachers always read books before using them in class!

In or outside class?

It is difficult to sustain interest in extensive reading. Many learners are reluctant to read without some element of teacher intervention. But reading in class is not the best use of limited class time, so we favour reading *outside* class with small but regular class slots for motivating interactive activities to sustain independent reading.

Some books are particularly suitable for class use, e.g. plays for acting out. Extracts from non-fiction books are often used in class in the same way as coursebook texts. This is particularly true of readers with strong specific subject content such as readers about business or science.

Finally ...

The debate revealed the enormous interest in graded readers, and their general acceptance as a valuable component of English language learning. It also showed the consensus among the series editors about what makes a good reader. What really surprised me in the current climate of interest in corpus-informed language learning is that so few publishers see the application to graded readers wordlists of the frequency information that they all proudly announce as underlying their dictionary content.

Philip Prowse *Freelance/CUP, England*

What makes a good graded reader? What is the question behind the question here? For me it's 'Why do we want good graded readers'? And the answer is obvious: to enable students to read with success and pleasure. Success and pleasure, because then students will continue to read, and we know that the surest indicator of language learning success is the habit of extensive reading.

But how do we provide this success and pleasure?

My starting point is language, because learning language is what it is all about. A good graded reader uses fresh, up-to-date language, vivid description and crisp dialogue, none of which betray the linguistic guidelines within which they are produced. Such an approach allows the reader at any level to focus on the story without hindrance. It takes great skill to achieve this and it is fatally easy to argue that adherence to wordlists and guidelines is unnecessary. I consider it (along with Paul Nation, who in *Learning Vocabulary in Another Language* (CUP 2001: 165) concludes that 'to gain adequate comprehension of the text most readers would need to know 98% of the running words in the text') to be fundamental. Moreover, any out-of-level words or phrases necessary to the story need to be contextualised, glossed within the story (not in a separate glossary), and repeated, so that the learner meets them again and again and is able to internalise them. Basically you can have the greatest story in the world, but that is no use if the learner cannot understand it.

We then move to content. Content not in the sense of story or plot, but of theme or topic. Successful fiction is 'about' something – it has themes and a depth which a potboiler lacks. Graded readers can deal with themes of love and family, of war and refugees, of personal identity and social crisis. A low language level is not to be equated with a low intellectual or emotional level. What is important is that the theme is of relevance to the learner now, so that she becomes engaged in it.

Cultural issues are also of great importance – those of you who were at the IATEFL conference in 2001 may recall the story of my attempts thirty years ago to teach a totally culturally unsuitable nineteenth-century novel (Arnold Bennett's *The Grand Babylon Hotel*) to groups of uncomprehending Egyptian teenagers. It is essential that a graded reader be accessible to the learner and not present barriers of cultural knowledge (whether it's a reference to Marks and Spencer, or an assumption of familiarity with behaviour at a social event) which the miscomprehending learner can attribute to lack of linguistic knowledge. In other words, we want the barriers down, and this can be successfully achieved by writing within a genre, so that the learner is placed in a familiar landscape and can predict what is likely to happen. One of the problems of adapting literature is that great literature often works by defying genre. That is why I am a firm believer in 'original' readers, not simplifications. A final cultural point is internationalism – by reading books set around the globe our learners achieve one of their aims in learning English – travel, albeit vicariously!

My fourth point relates not to the content of the graded reader but to its production values. My good graded reader looks like a real book – in other words it doesn't have a lot of comprehension questions at the back. It has excellent paper and print quality, and is accompanied by a really top-class recording.

Finally, of course, you need the 'turn the page' factor – the skill which keeps the reader reading!

Reflections on the debate

Three strong impressions remain from the debate.

Firstly it was clear that all four panellists were united in their passion for reading and graded readers. This unanimity of intent was significant in the message it sent about the importance of graded readers in language education – they are so ubiquitous that their presence and power can be forgotten (like chairs, the importance of which would only be realised were they to be removed). This unanimity was matched by sufficient diversity of opinion on how to produce graded readers to clearly differentiate the different series represented by their editors.

Secondly, the contributions solicited over the Web and skilfully synthesised by the Chair got the occasion off to an excellent start and stimulated contributions from the floor.

Thirdly, and perhaps inevitably, there wasn't time to do the Web and floor contributions justice and on some topics (certainly on vocabulary and word lists) I felt we were able to give less than adequate answers. However 75 minutes is still quite a long slot in conference terms for the 180 or so participants who attended.

To conclude: for me two messages emerged from the debate. The first is that there are many roads to heaven and that one must not be prescriptive about the use made of readers. While advocating pleasure reading as a goal, all the panellists were able to point to a wealth of supporting materials on websites and in worksheets for those teachers who wish to exploit a reader more intensively in class. The second is that the controversy over the relative superiority of original readers or simplifications is as much about cultural as linguistic values. It may well be that the cultural barriers presented by simplified 'classic' fiction tip the scales in favour of originals – but then the editor of a series of originals would say that, wouldn't he?

E-mail: cwalter@place-farm.demon.co.uk
s.axten@macmillan.com
jenny@daypotts.demon.co.uk
hopkinspotter@compuserve.com
philip.prowse@ntlworld.com

7 CONFERENCE REVIEWS

7.1 Language as a means of cultural transmission

Suliko Liiv *Tallinn University of Educational Sciences, Estonia*

Diane Larsen-Freeman's words in her plenary talk, 'Language is a means of cultural transmission, a means of interaction between and among people', very precisely characterised the atmosphere of the conference. The IATEFL conference brought together approximately 1,300 experts from over seventy countries to discuss topics of major interest about language learning and teaching.

I arrived in York just in time for the opening of registration, got my conference pack, and off I went to my room to get acquainted with all the practicalities. 'Don't forget that the stem of the word *conference* is to confer, so get out there and celebrate this special opportunity to confer with ELT professionals from all over the world', said Susan Barduhn in her introduction.

The venue for the conference was fantastic. York's unique buildings and fascinating medieval streets make it one of the most interesting towns in Britain. York University had kindly offered to host the conference on their campus, which enchanted us with its colourful daffodils, friendly ducks and rabbits. The best opportunity to enjoy that beauty was to sit and have lunch in the very heart of the beautiful campus and discuss issues of English language and English language teaching. The exchanges of impressions over the breakfast and dinner tables were very stimulating and added value to the whole event. To tell the truth, I would have liked to have more opportunities for personal contacts and networking among participants during the conference. There were bars open in the evening, but after working hard all day, plus jet lag, I was too tired to go to the pub! There were, as usual, evening events to meet all kinds of different tastes: comedy, a poetry reading, storytelling, and parties in medieval settings.

Diversification in modern language teaching and learning was among the key questions referred to by speakers. Varied presentations, hands-on sessions and wide-ranging discussions during the workshops produced a great deal of positive feedback. Participation in workshops was a particularly valuable experience and extremely important for the process of curricular renewal in my country.

The IATEFL conference is definitely an event not to be missed, as it offers teachers of EFL opportunities for professional development through the exchange of ideas in research and teaching English.

My special area of interest was teaching culture and therefore I tried to visit the workshops devoted to this topic or topics related to it. James Chamberlain's workshop 'Tools for training intercultural communication' examined various techniques and materials that trainers can use to facilitate intercultural communication training. Atsuko Watanabe and Rebecca Reagan's study about 'Issues of native vs. non-native teachers of English' was about advantages and disadvantages of each. Péter Medgyes' captivating workshop 'Laughing matters' was interspersed with 'fun' activities from the teacher's handbook of the same name, which I have now obtained.

Joanne Collie's and Antoinette Moses' session 'It's like what? Fact and fiction in cultural studies' examined two related questions: Is it important to include a comparative cultural dimension in language learning? and How can the study of fiction support the linguistic and cultural development of students of English? The inspiring performance of selected extracts from *Frozen Pizza,* generously donated to each participant and marvellously acted out by Antoinette Moses, the author of the book – to say nothing of the treat of real (not frozen!) slices of pizza at the CUP stand – made this session unforgettable.

Conferences are also places to meet 'big names'. It was a great pleasure and an honour for me to meet Michael Swan during his presentation of *The Good Grammar Book*, and I was happy that I got the authors' signatures in my personal copy of the book, and more importantly, that Michael Swan has now met somebody from Estonia.

I am particularly pleased to use this occasion to express my deepest appreciation to all those who ensured the smooth running of the conference and tried to cater to the needs of all the delegates.

7.2 Was it worth it?

Sue Morris *Freelance, Munich, Germany*

In her opening address, Susan Barduhn, the president of IATEFL, welcomed 1,200 delegates from a total of 77 countries. In the conference brochure she quoted Mojca Belak in the Teacher Development SIG Newsletter, who reminded us that 'every participant has something to offer, if you take some time and find out what you have in common with them.' Susan concluded her remarks by reminding us that the root of the word *conference* is 'to confer' and urged us to get out there and celebrate the opportunity to confer with ELT professionals from all over the world.

Well, I conferred with delegates from China, Finland, Hungary, Germany, Greece, Japan, Kosovo, the Netherlands and Sweden, as well as the UK. It was indeed refreshing to talk to new faces and hear their points of view. I wouldn't say that I made any new friends at IATEFL, but I did have time to talk to old ones over drinks. One friend I met purely by chance. We had been to school together and hadn't seen each other since 1974. IATEFL is like that. At my first conference in Manchester I met someone I had done my CELTA course with and also one whom I had worked with in Malaysia. This year I also had the pleasure of attending a friend's first-time presentation that went very well.

But IATEFL doesn't come cheap. So was it worth it? Was it more than just a pleasant social event, an opportunity to get the latest books at discount prices, and the chance to win free books and free courses at one of the 72 stands in the exhibition hall? It was not an encouraging beginning, as I almost didn't find my way to the registration desks in the exhibition building on the very attractive, if rather confusing, York University campus (attractive, that is, if you like ducks and can avoid their mess everywhere). However, I did get there in the end, so can answer these questions with a resounding 'yes'.

So why did I feel the organisers got it right for me this year? Because for me as a teacher, confidence and the feeling of getting it right at least most of the time, is very important. But what exactly do I mean by 'getting it right'? My lasting impression from this IATEFL conference was how difficult it is to answer this question for anyone but yourself and how comforting in some strange way this very uncertainty is. In one session in which participants were asked to make a model with Cuisenaire rods of how they saw learning, the group in which I found myself saw it as a journey along an ever-widening road. Teaching, I suggest, can be viewed in the same way. I am not suddenly going to choose another road, but insights gained at IATEFL help me become more aware and confident of how I am travelling along it.

My journey began with B. Kumaravadivelu's plenary session, in which he explained how teachers often have a knowledge of methods, but do not necessarily use a particular method in the classroom, showing the gulf that exists between theory and practice. His dissatisfaction with this situation has led him to suggest an alternative *to* method rather than an alternative method, but he also warned that knowledge and skill are needed if we are to be responsibly eclectic.

This idea of eclecticism set the tone for my experiences at the conference. The sessions that stood out for me were ones in which the speakers were supremely confident of what they were doing, but were undogmatic, were willing to show that they got it right most, but maybe not all of the time, that they too were on a journey. I have space to give my impressions of just three.

In Ronald Carter's talk entitled 'Language awareness revisited', he showed interesting examples from advertising and poetry and argued that discourse analysis is more than just awareness raising, as was believed in its infancy, but that it can develop thinking skills.

Dave Willis gave a very refreshing assessment of task-based learning (TBL) in contrast to presentation, practice and production (PPP). He held fast to his belief that the task should precede language work, as otherwise the students will do their best to do what they think the teacher wants to hear. However, he suggested that instead of arguing for PPP or TBL, we should take a closer look at what goes on in the classroom and decide which learning process is appropriate to what is being studied at the time.

The most stimulating session I went to was the plenary given by Diane Larsen-Freeman, delivered with erudition and wit, interspersed with rhetorical questions to keep us attentive. Had she been in the Cuisenaire rod session, her model of learning would have depicted participation. She explained language as a dynamic, fluid system, and that we use it as a tool to create knowledge. The language teacher's job, then, is not to focus on a code, but rather to respond respectfully to students' learning, as they attempt to understand the internal logic of this dynamic system in order to make their meaning clear.

As well as benefiting from their talks and workshops, you see the human side of the big names at an IATEFL conference. I saw Mario Rinvolucri sitting on the floor (in the absence of many places to sit on the York campus) in earnest conversation with a participant during a coffee break. I learnt that Mike McCarthy hates the noise of mobile phones as much as I do. I marvelled that Felicity O'Dell still found Mike McCarthy's talk as interesting as I did, even though she co-authors books on vocabulary with him. I gained respect for big names as I noticed how they attended each other's sessions, showing that they still have things to learn, just like you and me.

There is always innovation at the IATEFL conference. This year's innovation was an open forum between publishers and writers, in which the 'creativity versus profit' dichotomy was aired. I didn't stay for the whole three hours, but long enough to hear two things that made me think. Firstly, Péter Medgyes' plea to writers (in his case to non-native speakers, but it could apply to anyone) to accept criticism with an open heart and secondly, to hear Mario Rinvolucri's assessment that in the age of e-publishing, editors are more than ever needed to act as a filter for an author's arrogance.

So, yes, it was worth it. Of all the sessions that I attended, only one was a complete waste of time and that was a 20-minute slot, a daunting prospect indeed for anyone. Sessions were mostly 50 minutes, long enough for presenters to make their points well. I chose carefully this year, combining talks with workshops, ones that I thought would be really useful to me and ones that I thought might simply be fun. It can be mind-numbing to go to too many talks, when one just sits passively. Workshops allow you to talk to others, bounce ideas off them and gain the confidence that you are getting it right some of the time.

I hope you come to Brighton next year and get it right!